Taqwiyat-ul-Iman

Strengthening of the Faith

Shah Ismail Shaheed

CONTENTS

1. Publisher's Note
2. Preface
3. Prelude

Chapter One

Description of *Tauhid*

4. People's unawareness
5. The acts leading to polytheism
6. Those who profess to have Faith in Allah while their actions reeking of polytheism
7. The verdict of Qur'an
8. None but Allah is the Capable
9. None is the supporter other than Allah
10. None is the sustainer other than Allah
11. The reality of *Shirk*

Chapter Two

Categories and aspects of *Shirk*

12. *Shirk* in knowledge
13. *Shirk* in disposing
14. *Shirk* in worship
15. *Shirk* in one's daily routine chores

Chapter Three

The Vices of Polytheism

The Virtues of Monotheism

16. The polytheism cannot be forgiven
17. Explaining *Shirk*
18. *Shirk*, the greatest of all vices
19. *Tauhid* is the only way out
20. Allah is disgusted with *Shirk*
21. Affirming the Oneness of Allah prior to the dawn of time itself
22. *Shirk* cannot be presented as an authority
23. The excuse of forgetfulness shall not be accepted
24. The basic teachings of the Prophets and the Scriptures
25. *Tauhid* and forgiveness

Chapter Four

The negation of *Shirk* in knowledge

26. Only Allah possess the knowledge of *Ghaib*
27. The one who claims to have the knowledge of *Ghaib,* is a liar
28. The matters of *Ghaib*
29. Do not call upon anyone but Allah
30. Allah Alone, possesses the power of benefit and inflicting harm
31. The original assignment of the Prophets
32. The Prophets do not have the knowledge of unseen

33. The saying of the Prophet {Peace be upon Him} regarding the knowledge of the unseen
34. The saying of Aisha{Peace be upon Her}

Chapter Five

The Negation of *Shirk* in Authority

35. Allah is the One Who causes benefit and inflicts harm
36. None is the sustainer except Allah
37. Invoke none but Allah
38. No intercession without His Permission
39. Types of intercession
40. An intercession due to one's high-ranking status is not possible
41. Acceptance of one's intercession out of love is not possible
42. Interceding with permission
43. The Straight Path
44. Allah is the Nearest to all
45. Trust in Allah Alone
46. Relationship does not benefit

Chapter Six

Prohibition of *Shirk* in Worship

47. The definition of worship
48. Worship is meant for Allah Alone
49. Prostration is for Allah only
50. It is an act of *Shirk* to call upon other than Allah
51. The holy sanctuaries must be respected
52. Anything dedicated to an entity other than Allah is forbidden
53. Authority and command is only for Allah
54. Giving someone false names is an act of *Shirk*
55. So-called customs are acts of *Shirk*
56. Keeping people stand up in one's honor is prohibited
57. Worshipping idols and the so-called "sanctums of saints" is an act of *Shirk*
58. Slaughtering an animal in a name other than that of Allah is a curse
59. Indications heralding the advent of Doomsday
60. Worshipping the places of saints is an act of the worst people
61. Performing *Tawaf* of the idols

Chapter Seven

Prohibition of *Shirk* in Social Customs

62. The whispering of Satan
63. Polytheistic rituals in regard to the soliciting of children
64. Polytheistic rituals in agriculture
65. Polytheistic rituals in regard to the cattle
66. Slandering Allah in the matters of lawful and forbidden things
67. Giving credit to the influence of planets is an act of *Shirk*
68. The astrologers are magicians and the magicians are Disbelievers
69. The sin of believing in astrology

70. Deducing an omen is an act of disbelief
71. Do not make Allah an Intercessor
72. The dearest names to Allah
73. *Kunya* with the Name of Allah must be avoided
74. Only say *MashaAllah*
75. Taking an oath in the name of anyone other than Allah is an act of *Shirk*
76. The verdict of the Prophet {peace be upon Him} about observing vows
77. Prostration to Allah and paying due respect to a Messenger
78. It is not permissible to call someone one's slave
79. An excellent example to pay respect to the Prophet {Peace be upon Him}
80. The word *Saiyid* carries two meanings
81. Sayings of the Prophet {Peace be upon Him} in regard to the pictures
82. The five major sins
83. The statement of the Prophet {Peace be upon Him} about himself

Publisher's Note

At a time when the general milieu in the subcontinent of India was overwhelmed by the powers of darkness, and the soundness of Faith was reeling under the potentially threatening squalls and the blinding forages of superstitions and paganism, Allah the Almighty, by dint of His special blessing, sent a personality, who, by the strength of his Faith, knowledge and rhetoric, dissipated the redoubtable forces of depravity and smashed the self-made idols of *Shirk* (polytheism) and *Bid'ah* (innovations in religion) and established the base of pure *Tauhid* (Islamic Monotheism). This great personality was Shah Ismail Muhaddith Dehlawi {May Allah have mercy on him}, who was the grandson of Shah Waliullah Dehlawi, a man of profound knowledge and great name to be reckoned with in terms of his authentic scholarship among the most qualified and famous celebrities of his time. The services which he has rendered for the reformation of *Ummah* and his undertaking the task of *Da'wah* (the mission of propagating Islam); especially after the previous works of Shaikhul-Islam Imam Ibn Taimiyah and Muhammad bin AbdulWahhab, are absolutely unforgettable and shall always be cherished in our minds. His status is specially far more prominent and elevated due to the fact that he not only carried on with his struggle on the strength of his pen and tongue, but he practically joined *Tahreek-ul-Mujahidin* (the first Islamic *Mujahid* movement) under the inspiring leadership of Saiyid Ahmad Shaheed and achieved martyrdom in his armed struggle against the Sikhs at Balakot and hence set an ideal example for the weak, incapacitated and oppressed Muslims of India.

The age of Shah Ismail Shaheed was infested and contaminated with the poisonous atmosphere of *Shirk* and innovations. The Indian Muslims, under the influence of the Hindu mythological faith, had entered such rituals and beliefs in Islam that they even surpassed the ones observed during the pre-Islamic period (in terms of their polytheistic rituals).

Taking the above facts into consideration, Shah Ismail Shaheed's religious sense of honor and the integrity of his Faith could not tolerate the spectacle that Islam which has been choiced for the slaves of Allah to confirm His Oneness (which is also the purpose of affirming one's faith in the Prophethood), should be infiltrated with and gnawed by the concept of associating partners to Allah. In order to achieve this august and noble purpose, he compiled *Taqwiyat-ul-Iman* (the strengthening of faith), wherein he, along with construing and elaborating on Qur'an and *Ahadith,* also expatiated at length about the pure Islamic beliefs, and declaring all the innovations and rituals the source of ignorance in the light of Qur'an and *Sunnah,* he emphatically enjoined upon the Muslims to avoid being involved with them. Apart from bearing such exalted and elevated aims, this book, on account of its elegant, breezy, simple and elaborate style of prose (according to the requirement of its age), proved to be so much popular among the peoples that it has so far been published in millions and has enlightened trillions of delinquent and strayed people and has guided them to the Right Path.

It must be brought to the attention of our readers that a preface written by Maulana Ghulam Rasool Mehr (the late), encompassing an eloquent description and a mighty rhetoric on the comprehensive benefits and profitability of *Taqwiyat-ul-Iman* is also included in this book and hence we presume that writing anything further in this regard shall be amounting to proverbially carrying coals to Newcastle.

However, the only thing we would like to add here is, that this book is being published with all its former qualitative characteristics along with the corrections and castigations effected by Moulana (the late).

However, some minor changes in words and style have been made keeping in line with the call of time. We are optimistic that the readers of this book shall be kind enough to tolerate these changes, as the same shall make it a lot easier for them to understand the facts which this book comprises.

However, we have spared no effort in making *Taqwiyat-ul-Iman* more presentable and appealing to our readers. May Allah bless us with a guidance to be led on the Right Path. *Amin.*

The Servant of Qur'an and Sunnah
Abdul-Malik Mujahid
General Manager

PREFACE

Shah Muhammad Ismail {May Allah have mercy on him} the author of *Taqwiyat-ul-.Iman* was the solitary son of Shah Abdul-Ghani {May Allah have mercy on him}, the grandson of Shah Waliullah Muhaddith Dehlawi {May Allah have mercy on him}, and the nephew of Shah Abdul Aziz Muhaddith {May Allah have mercy on him}, Shah Rafiuddin Muhaddith {May Allah have mercy on him} and Shah Abdul-Qadir Muhaddith {May Allah have mercy on him}.In the vast Indian subcontinent, no one else other than Shah Ismail perhaps enjoys such a high and respectable pedigree in terms of knowledge and grace, teaching and instructing, writing and compiling, lecturing and prompting guidance, reinvigorating and renewing the teachings of religion, reviving Islam and reforming the *Ummah*. Very few people may have had a privilege of getting such a rich and spectacular heritage. Shah Ismail Shaheed {May Allah have mercy on him} not only lived up to the great reputation and enormity of his legacy, but he practically furthered its splendor manifold times and added luster to it.

According to an authentic source, Shah Ismail {May Allah have mercy on him} was born on 12th Rabi'ul-Awwal 1193 H (corresponding to 26th April 1779 G). It means that he was almost seven years older than his religious preceptor and mentor, the *Amir-ul-Muminin* (the head of the believers) Saiyid Ahmad Barailawi {May Allah have mercy on him}. The name of his mother was Bibi Fatimah {May Allah have mercy on her}.[1]

1

] Mir Shahamat Ali, in the preface of his English translation of *Taqwiyat ul-Iman*, has mentioned his date of birth as 28th of Shawwall195 H. And has stated his mother's name as Fadeelat-un-Nisa (daughter of Moulvi Alauddin Phulti). His maternal ancestry undoubtedly belonged to Phulat and his sister Bibi Ruqaiya's first marriage to his maternal cousin Moulvi Kamaluddin did take place in Phulat itself, but the authentic statement regarding his date of birth and the name of his mother is the one which is recorded in the 'text. We do not know about the source of his reference. He has mentioned several other things in his biography which are incorrect.

Education & training:

Shah Sahib attained his preliminary education from his esteemed father. At the tender age of eight, he had memorized the Noble Qur'an. On 16th of Rajab 1203 H (12th April 1789 G), Shah Abdul Ghani {May Allah have mercy upon him} passed away while Shah Shaheed was only 10 years old. Each of his three paternal uncles (Shah Abdul-Aziz {May Allah have mercy upon him} Shah Rafiuddin {May Allah have mercy on him} and Shah Abdul-Qadir{May Allah have mercy on him} were equally keen to affectionately take charge of upbringing their bereaved nephew, but this responsibility was formally shouldered by Shah Abdul-Qadir {May Allah have mercy on him} who himself had only one daughter. He is the one who taught the text books to Shah Ismail {May Allah have mercy on him.. He attained a degree of proficiency in all the prescribed subjects which were then in vogue and which were considered to be the highest standard of education one could possibly secure those days. He secured a degree of completion in the studies of *Ahadith* from Shah Abdul-Aziz {May Allah have mercy on him} and thus he completed his education while he was about 15 or 16 years old.

According to Sir Saiyid Ahmad Khan, he was so much overconfident in the very beginning stage of his studies that he would never remember as to where the lesson would really start. Sometimes he would start reading the text which immediately followed his present lesson. Whenever Shah Abdul-Qadir interrupted him such as to remind him of his actual lesson, he would answer that he avoided it since it was too easy for him, and whenever Shah Abdul-Qadir would ask him any question concerning the portion which he had skipped, he would start delivering such an eloquent lecture about it that the people around him would be taken aback by surprise. Sometimes he would start his lesson proceeding the one which he is supposed to read and when Shah Abdul-Qadir brought his attention to it, he would express such doubts that even an accomplished instructor like him would have to pay a special attention in responding to his querries.

His extraordinary intelligence became renowned far and wide. After he had completed his formal studies, people would put direct querries to him even while he was walking on the road simply to examine him, keeping in mind the fact that so long as he did not have a book in his hand, he would not be able to give satisfactory answers to their querries. But Shah Ismail 'Nould unhesitatingly start lecturing them and provide such a detailed answer to their querries that they would be ultimately put to shame on their boldness.

Maulana Muhammad Khan Alam Madrasi has written on the authority of Maulana Saiyid Muhammad Ali Rampuri's statement that Shah Shaheed was a scholar of a very deep, profound, and authentic knowledge and had memorized the Noble Qur'an by heart. He had thirty thousand *Ahadith* on the tip of his tongue.

Saiyid Sahib's {May Allah have mercy on him} *Bai'a* (pledge):

Even though Shah Shaheed's fame in terms of his learning and wisdom had traveled far and wide, but he was a man of a rather carefree disposition, which means that he had not adopted an occupation on a permanent basis, the reason of which could possibly be that the activities which were practiced by his family members, might have been inadequately suited for the reforming purpose according to his viewpoint, while he had no other new activity in his frame of mind. Or it could be that he would have had set his heart on a certain course of action and was only waiting in search of companions and fellows.

In. 1234 H (1819 G) *Amirul-Muminin* (the head of the believers) Saiyid Ahmad Barailawy {May Allah have mercy on him} abandoned the company of Nawab Amir Khan, the ruler of Tounk proceeded to Delhi from Rajputana and took residence in Akbar Abadi Mosque. The first to take a pledge of allegiance on his hand was Maulana Muhammad Yusuf Phulti, who was presumably a grandson of Shah Ahlullah, a brother of Shah Waliullah {May Allah have mercy on him}.The second person to take such a pledge on his blessed hand was Maulana Abdul-Hai {May Allah have mercy on him} (the son-in-law of Shah Abdul-Aziz {May Allah have mercy on him}and finally it was Shah Shaheed who took a pledge on his hand. Once he did it, his life underwent a total transformation. He became obsessed with the task of reformation and guidance day and night. On every Tuesday and Friday, he regularly delivered a religious lecture in Shahi Masjid (Royal Mosque). Sir Saiyid says in one of his writings that the people came to the Friday prayers in such a huge number, as if they throng the mosques for the *'Eid* prayers in the form of a massive and thundering crowd. Their number was phenomenal and innumerable. The method of his sermonizing was so pleasing that whatever he said, got ingratiated in the hearts of the people and they imbibed it to the core. Even if it involved a snag or a controversial point the same was cleared away during the course of his sermon. Revival of *Sunnah* and deterring *Shirk* (polytheism) and *Bid'ah* (innovations) were the special subjects of his religious lectures. This was the time when the mission of the revival of religion commenced in full swing with all its might. This was the era about which Maulana Abul-Kalam Azad {May Allah have mercy on him}notes the following remarks in his book *Tadhkirah:*

"The secrets of (the mission of) *Da'wah* (i.e. call to Islam) and reformation of *Ummah* that were buried in the ruins of Old Delhi and the hovels and shanties of Kotla, were now being revived thanks to the involvement of the reigning sovereign, which caused a wave of consternation in the markets of Shahjahanabad and an uproar on the stairs of *Jami' Masjid* by this great and distinguished person. Not only that, the news transcended the boundaries of the Indian subcontinent but had it's repercussions far and wide. The things which the great and renowned personalities of their time would not dare to express even inside the closed rooms, were now being said, heard and practiced in the open without reserve and the blood of martyrdom was indenting its indelible imprints and inscribing its redoubtable saga in the annals of the world history."

The pilgrimage journey:

In Shawwal 1236 (July 1821 G), Saiyid Ahmad {May Allah have mercy on him}intended to perform *Hajj*. Taking into account the possibility of death during a sea-journey, many scholars had pronounced their judgments to the effect that the performance of *Hajj* is no longer to be considered of an obligatory nature. Some people even went to the extent of saying that according to the commandment of the Qur'anic verse:

{**And not throw yourselves into destruction**}

The purpose of *Hajj* is nothing but the disobedience of Allah (May Allah forbid!). One of the methods which could be employed to checkmate this evil trend was through one's writings, verbal preachings, and therefore Saiyid Sahib, Shah Ismail{May Allah have mercy on him}, Maulana Abdul-Hai {May Allah have mercy on him}Shah Abdul-Aziz {May Allah have mercy on him} and the righteous scholars did not leave any stone unturned in regard to this obligation of theirs. Another method was to subject the atmosphere of this vast country to the barrage of a positive publicity in regard to the performance of *Hajj* by taking a practical course of action in order to awaken and revive the public fervor interest and enthusiasm in it. Saiyid Ahmad {May Allah have mercy on him} was a man of determination and courage, who undoubtedly acted upon the second method also, the most surprising part of it being that he directed an open invitation for *Hajj* to all the Muslims of the country. He made a common declaration to the effect that everybody should be prepared to perform the pilgrimage whether or not he has sufficient funds available with him for the journey. He took it upon himself to shoulder a comprehensive responsibility for everybody's *Hajj*. He not only preserved the obligatory nature of *Hajj* in its original form in the minds of people but also practically demonstrated to them that this obligation may be performed at ease, provided one should be determined to perform it as a Divine commandment with the intention of a true and sincere Muslim.

Therefore, it followed that Saiyid Ahmad proceeded to perform *Hajj* with a caravan consisting of seven hundred and fifty Muslims. He was also accompanied by Shah Shaheed, his esteemed mother, and his sister. They rented ten ships, assigned an *Amir* to each ship to look after the affairs of the pilgrims traveling aboard them and commenced their journey from Calcutta. After the completion of their *Hajj* and having visited all the sacred places, they came back in Sha'ban 1239 H (April 1824 G). During this journey, Shah Ismail {May Allah have mercy on him} was appointed as an *Amir* over a group of people traveling aboard one of the ships.

Invitation to *Jihad*:

Upon his return from the pilgrimage, Shah Shaheed {May Allah have mercy on him} dedicated himself wholeheartedly for the sole purpose of inviting people to *Jihad* as per the instructions of his religious preceptor. Sir Saiyid in one of his writings says:

"According to the instructions of his chief, leader of the virtuous ones and preceptor of the path of guidance, he adopted such a style of speech and sermonizing that it mainly elaborated on the details and explanations concerning *Jihad* in Allah's course to such an extent that the burnishing effect of his speeches made the inner conscience of Muslims clean and immaculate like a mirror. He became so much involved and dedicated to this cause of righteousness that everybody was involuntarily intrigued with a longing that his life be sacrificed for this esteemed cause of virtuosity and his whole self be exerted for the upliftment of religion of Prophet Muhammad {Peace be upon Him}.

Migration:

He spent more or less one year and nine months in the task of his invitations to *Jihad*. When different groups of *Mujahidin* were formed at different places, it was decided after due exchange of thoughts and deliberations that *Jihad* should be commenced starting from the frontier region where the Sikh government of the Punjab had started committing aggressions. On 7th Jumada-al-Ukhra 1241 H (17th January 1826 G), Shah Shaheed {May Allah have mercy on him} commenced his migration on his way to *Jihad*. Then he was accompanied by only 500 or 600 people. It was decided that once they reached the prescribed centre, they would first run an appraisal on the prevalent circumstances and then the remaining groups would be called in. During this journey, Shah Shaheed was bearing a special responsibility of the administrative matters in general as well as being a flag-bearer of the targets concerning the mission of propagating Islam.

This group commenced its journey from Rai Baraili and went all the way to Peshawar via Bundhail Khand, Gwallior, Tonk, Ajmer, the desert of Marwar, Umar Kot, Hyderabad (Sind), Shikarpur, Quetta, Qandhar, Ghazni and Kabul. It was about three thousand miles journey comprising searing deserts where there was no trace of water for miles and miles, big and mighty rivers, intractable mountains as well as frosty landscape. It took ten months to cover all this distance.

Jihad:

Jihad with sword (i.e. the armed struggle) commenced on the 20th of Jumada-al-ula 1242 H (20th December 1826 G). The following is a brief account of his most specific and salient accomplishments:

1. It is only due to his efforts that the people of the frontier region gave the pledge of allegiance on the hands of Saiyid Sahib concerning *Jihad*. Most of the deliberations which were conducted with the religious scholars and the elderly in the frontier region were initiated by Shah Shaheed.

2. He is the one who organized the matters concerning *Jihad* in the district of Hazara. Even though he had only ten or eleven *Mujahidin* in the battle of Shankiyari at his command, yet he convincingly vanquished over a fairly huge legion of Sikh army by displaying a feat of extraordinary perseverance and steadfastness. During the course of this battle, Shah Shaheed's robe got perforated with bullets and one of his fingers got bruised by a gunshot. Later he would point to his finger in a good humor and jocularly remark (by playing a pun on words) "This is my finger of martyrdom." (This very expression, with a twist of the linguistic pun, would also mean, "This is my finger of witnessing that there is no one worthy of being worshipped except Allah and Muhammad{Peace be upon Him})

3. It is only due to his efforts that the people were prepared to take an oath of allegiance in regard to the observance of *Shari'ah* in their day-to-day lives and the people of the frontier region enjoyed the blessings and bounties of a government based on the principles of Islamic law.

4. It was under his leadership that the prominent victories were achieved in the battles of Amb, Ashrah, Mardan and Mayar. After the conquest of Peshawar, Saiyid Sahib nominated none other than him to conduct negotiations with Sultan Muhammad Khan Barak Zai. Due to the recalcitrance of the opportunistic elements in the frontier region, the circumstances therein got extremely deteriorated and threateningly adverse and when Saiyid Sahib took a decision to abandon this centre and proceeded to Kashmir through the intractable and difficult route traversing and winding through the mountainous landscape, he was also accompanied by Shah Shaheed in this journey.

5. During their journey to Kashmir, a battle at Balakot on 24th Dhil-Qa'dah 1246 H (6th May 1831 G) took place wherein Saiyid Sahib, Shah Shaheed and the majority of *Mujdhidin* attained their martyrdom.

A glimpse of his biography:

As far as we could understand by looking at his biography, Shah Shaheed never liked formalities in the matters of his day-to-day living. Upon being accompanied with Saiyid Ahmad, he became so much gleeful and carefree within his lowest standard of living as if he was seated on the throne of an emperor. When he reached Calcutta while being emote to his pilgrimage, the agent of East India Company, Munshi Aminuddin Ahmad came to visit him. During his time, he was considered to be one of the rich and famous personalities of Calcutta. After meeting Saiyid Ahmad, he enquired of him concerning the whereabouts of Shah Ismail {May Allah have mercy on him}. At that very moment, he was walking towards Saiyid Ahmad after having alighted from the ship. His clothes were all besmeared with dirt. When the people beaconed in his direction, Munshi Aminuddin was under the impression that he would have been some other Ismail. In order to clarify himself further, he reiterated his question saying, "The person I am enquiring about is Shah Ismail {May Allah have mercy on him} who is the nephew of Shah Abdul-Aziz {May Allah have mercy on him}. When he was told that this very person is the one he was looking for, he was so much moved to observe his simplicity in disposition and informality in manners that he involuntarily turned emotional and burst into tears.

Saiyid Ahmad gave a horse to Shah Ismail so that he may use it as a means of transport, but whenever he went out to run an errand for himself, he made one of his colleagues mount on it while he himself preferred to walk on foot on the plea that so long as we are out on a religious mission, the more we bear the hardships, the more virtues we shall accrue to our credit.

His faithful attachment to Saiyid Ahmad is a renowned fact. People have spun many a yam in regard to his attachment with him. Regardless whether these stories are true or false, there is no denying the fact that Shah Ismail had a very deep and extraordinary attachment with Saiyid Ahmad. In spite of all this, his faith in him never had any bearing on his truthfulness as he never hesitated to say the right thing. On one occasion, the Amb Fort, which sheltered Saiyid Ahmad's family and the other ladies, was threatened with an imminent danger. Saiyid Ahmad wrote a letter to Shah Ismail instructing him to convey the ladies out to a safe place so that the *Mujdhidin* do not have to come across any possible difficulty during the course of their battle. Shah Ismail had a notion that the ouster of ladies from there would have an adverse effect on the morals of the people ~round them as the same shall be interpreted by them to be a presentiment of a lurking disaster. Therefore, it was conveyed to Saiyid Ahmad that this action at this juncture would be untimely and hence inadvisable. When Saiyid Ahmad reiterated his instructions, Shah Ismail wrote to him in no uncertain terms that the compliance with his instructions shall only harm Muslims and therefore he alone shall be answerable about it on the Day of Judgment. Upon hearing this Saiyid Ahmad took his orders back.

Even though he was not that old, but a study of the events covering his last days reveals that his physique had grown extremely weak and emaciated as a result of his being constantly subjected to the rigorous and laborious work which he kept rendering for the sake of religion. On one occasion, he insistently made a small cannon mounted on his shoulders in order to awaken the spirit of determination among the people, but his feet started shaking and staggering about due to the burden. While climbing a mountain, he would start panting profusely just after clambering his way up a few steps, but despite having been in this enfeebled condition, it never happened till the last moment that he would ever lag behind anyone in taking an active part in a battle or in the matter of undertaking a journey. He would never even slacken to cover up two days journey in one day whenever the same was required of him, keeping in view the realization of the desired objectives of the war. On several occasions, in the frontier region, he had to come to grips with the religious, martial and political problems of a crucial nature and Shah Ismail kept resolving them with an effortless ease. A famous chronicle had it that while he was once busy in curry-combing a horse, some people enquired of him concerning some religious matters. He kept curry-combing his horse while responding to the queries of his interlocutors to the fullest.

Saiyid Jafar Ali Naqwi writes that once he had an opportunity to be led by him in one of his prayers. In a prayer consisting of two *Rak'a,* he recited the complete *'Surah* Bani Israel' in such a mystifying and spiritually enlightening manner that he never ever derived such a blissful and heart-felt pleasure behind any *Imam* till the moment of writing. He writes that he will never ever forget that particular prayer in his lifetime.

Is there any who will remember (or receive admonition):

It was Shah Ismail {May Allah have mercy on him}who exerted every moment of his life in upholding the word of truth and the revival of Islam. He is the one who sacrificed all his worldly pleasures in the service of religion without the least hesitation and demonstrated the sincerity of his mission by the blood of his martyrdom. In case we are courageous enough to gauge the ratings of our Faith in Allah and run an unbiased appraisal on the quality of our religious integrity, where shall we all stand? How unfortunate it is that hundreds of the so-called and self-proclaimed 'saints' occupying their seats and sanctum sanctorums inside the shrines of the erstwhile saints in the name of religion, have been heaping curses, on this great scholar and *Mujahid,* constantly for a period of hundred and twenty-five years. They did not only eye his love of Islam with suspicion, but doubted his Islam itself. We are listened to these curses and abuses with such a great interest and enthusiasm, as if it was a unique heroic deed and requisite to preserve and safeguard one's religion and piety.

Children:

Shah Abdul-Qadir conducted Shah Shaheed's matrimony with his grand-daughter Bibi Kulthum. He sired only one child whose name was Shah Muhammad Umar, who spent all his life in an absorbed state (as if lost in meditation).

His works:

Shah Ismail Shaheed has several works to his credit. Here are some of them to name a few:

1. A treatise on the principles of *Fiqh* (Islamic jurisprudence) which has been published.
2. A treatise on logic which has been referred to, by Sir Saiyid Ahmad Khan.
3. A book titled "Clarifying the evident truth about the rulings concerning the dead and the shrines." Experts observe that no book, the like of, has ever been written in any language which brings into limelight the reality of *Bid'ah* (inventing new things in religion). Regrettably, this work could not have been completed. This has been published twice or thrice along with its Urdu translation.
4. "The Status and Dignity of an *Imam."* This too is an excellent book. The Persian manuscripts are very rare now, however Urdu versions are available.
5. "Illuminating the two eyes in regard to the raising of hands." This is the collection of those *Ahadith* which prove that the raising of hands (as prescribed during a prayer) is an act of *Sunnah* (supererogatory). This book has been published many times with its Urdu version. Its Arabic edition has recently been published along with the explanatory notes by *Jamiat-e-Ahle-Hadith, Pakistan* (The Department for the Propagation of *Sunnah)* in an

extremely elegant style.[1]

6. "The Straight Path." This book has four chapters. Only the first chapter has been written by Shah Shaheed. The contents of it all have originally been written by Saiyid Sahib, whereas the expressions and the style of writing belong to Shah Sahib. Its Urdu version has also been published. Its Persian version was only published once and is now very rarely available.[2]

7. *"Taqwiyat-ul-Iman"* (the strengthening of Faith), the details of which follow further ahead.

8. *Yak-Rozi* (One dayer), is a short treatise in which Moulvi Fadl Haq Khairabadi's objections on his book *Taqwiyat-ul-Iman* have been answered. While Shah Sahib was on his way to the mosque to perform his prayer, he received the letter of Moulvi Fadl Haq. Immediately after offering his prayer, he sat down to write an answer to it and finished it in one stroke. This is why it has been named *Yak Rozi*.

9. *Makateeb* (The written notes), is one of his very big collections. Some of them became quite well-known in his name. He wrote most of them on the instigation of Saiyid Sahib.

10. His verified works which are as follows
    - A Persian *Qaseedah* (panegyric) in praise of the Prophet{Peace be upon Him}
    - A Persian *"Qaseedah"'* (panegyric) praising Saiyid Sahib.
    - A Persian *Mathnawi* (long narrative poem) known as *Silk-e-Noor* (a thread of light) on the subject of *Tauhid* (The Oneness of Allah).
    - An Urdu *Mathnawi* (long narrative poem) also on the subject of *Tauhid*.
    - A Persian *Mathnawi* (long narrative poem) in explanation of a *Hadith*.

The history of *Taqwiyat-ul-Iman*:

Taqwiyat-ul-Iman was first published in 1242 (1826-27 G) at the time when Shah Saheed, Saiyid Ahmad Barailawi {May Allah have mercy on him} had migrated along with a group of *Mujahidin* from their beloved native land and an armed struggle *(Jihad)* was about to take place for the liberation and purification of India. Within a period of last 170 years, we can not say with any degree of certainty as to how many times it has so far been published. However, we presume by employing a rough guess that the same must have been published at least four or five million copies! Trillions of people have been enlightened by reading it. This is such a dignity which perhaps no other book of Urdu language other than *Taqwiyat-ul-Iman* has the honor of achieving so far. A blizzard of misgivings and a string of diatribe which was unleashed against this book has been seldom witnessed by any other book. If we look at the history of

Taqwiyat-ul-Iman today, a strange spectacle materialises in our imagination, as if it is an ocean being rocked by the fury of a hurricane, it's surface being constantly lashed by the tumult, anguish, friction and tempestuousness of its broken waves, thereby giving it a great resemblance with the Day of Judgment. Dejection is writ large on the faces of the captains of all the colossal and Herculean ships and they are all anchored firmly sticking on to the sea-shore. However, there is only one courageous navigator who, despite the fragility of his ship, is still keeping his ship continuously asail. He is a person of such an unflinching Faith and solidity that all the ravages

---

[1] *'Al-Maktabah As-Salafiyah'* has also published its translated version.
[2] This has now *Alhamdulillah* been published by *Al-Maktabah As-Salafiyah*

and depredations fail to produce a single favoring grimace of fidgeting on his eyebrow. All those atrocities and redouble furies of the hurricane who had forced all the sea stalwarts and the old salts to dock their ships by the sea-shore the equally forbidding and threatening in intimidating this very daunting navigator, but he, for the sake of his sense of duty and compliance, braves and defies them. This navigator kept advancing further ahead thwarting and frustrating all the forces who are at work in his opposition and thus becomes entitled to such a position of honor which only fall to the lot of the ones exhibiting forbearance and patience.

The salient features of this book:

The subject matter of *Taqwiyat-ul-Iman* is *Tauhid* (the Oneness of Allah), which is the foundation and the basis of religion. Innumerable books and treatises have so far been written on this topic, but the style of Shah Shaheed and his technique of the subject treatment is the most outstanding and unique one and is purely reformatory. He made only Qur'an and *Sunnah* the orbit of his discussion just like the righteous scholars. He proffers and refers to the Qur'anic verses and *Ahadith* and interprets them in a very simple and comprehensible style and brings to light the true status of all the unlawful customs and rituals, which are commonly practiced in the society and are detrimental to the faith of *Tauhid* (Islamic Monotheism) in a very pleasant and impressive style.

He gathered under different topics all the horrible blunders of Faith and practice which are contrary to teaching of Islamic Monotheism, for instance, committing an act of *Shirk* (associating partners to Allah) in terms of knowledge, regulating the affairs of the universe, habits and practices and *Shirk* in worshipping. Hence *Taqwiyat-ul-Iman* has become an authentic and unique book on the subject of *Tauhid*. In addition to the above, it also attempts to highlight the following:

1. This book is an extremely surprising specimen, giving us an insight into the educational, practical and cultural patterns which were in vogue during the times of Shah Shaheed. If someone intends to have a background information as to what were the dogmatic, practiced and moral ailments which the Muslims were suffering from in this vast country before one hundred and thirty years, this book shall prove to be an excellent source of information for him.

2. Shah Shaheed did not make himself contented with the task of merely elucidating the intricacies of the theoretical precepts of *Tauhid* but he rather assumed such a style of writing which makes reader mentally conjure up a picture of that society and its surrounding milieu in which that book had been written. This potentially enhances the efficacy and effectiveness of *Da'wah* (Call to Islam).

3. Even though this book covers an extremely important subject, but Shah Shaheed adopted such a method of reasoning and deducing facts that both a slightly educated as well as an extremely educated person, according to their own intellectual standards of perception, may and have been benefiting from the said book.

4. Even though this book was written during a period when the Urdu prose-writing was developing through its preliminary stages, but Shah Sahib's prose is so simple, breezy, fresh and pleasing that, except a few words and idioms, it is not simple even today to write such a fascinating book. This is an undemiable fact that even though the Urdu language has progressed through the additional phases of its development, it will always

consider *Taqwiyat-ul-Iman* to be an invaluable treasure in terms of stylistics.

The opposite attitudes of respect and neglect:

It is an extremely amazing phenomenon that even though *Taqwiyat-ul-Iman,* is replete with a host of advantages, it has been subjected to an ambivalent attitude on the part of its devotees, as this book, on one hand was well taken care of, while on the other hand, it was thrown into neglect too at the same time. People paid such a tremendous attention to its publication and distribution that no other book in Urdu language could rival it. It has been the practice of many people and organizations that they used to publish thousands of its copies annually and distributed it either gratis or against a very nominal charge, while on the other hand, it was neglected to such an extent that no castigation or correction was ever effected in it. No one even cared about getting it serialized under different chapters or producing it in a more polished and presentable shape keeping in view the ever changing tastes and proclivities of the readers. It seems as if the devotees of this book have merely given it a sanctified status, limiting their association and attachment with this book to the extent of preserving it and handing it over in its original and unabridged form to the oncoming generations. According to my knowledge, there have been only two attempts so far in regard to the correction of the text and entering footnotes to it on two different occasions, but they two were not accomplished in a full-fledged manner.

Essential tasks:

There have been many essential tasks which may not be hidden from the eyes of the people who have a refined taste in compiling and publishing. A study of *Taqwiyat-ul-Iman* at once reveals that Shah Shaheed, just similar to his other works, also wrote it at once and in a single effort. Since he had devoted his life to the great cause of the Islamic revival whole-heartedly to the extent that he had hardly any time left for other activities, he did not have an opportunity to review his manuscript of *Taqwiyat-ul-Iman* either. The essential task concerning this book which Shah Shaheed could not undertake to accomplish by himself, his devotees were supposed to do the needful by themselves. For instance, they could have effected the following changes:

1. They could have got the book properly synchronized and serialized under different titles and sub-titles to render it easier for the readers as well as to make it more fruitful and informative for them.
2. Shah Sahib, according to his requirement, had only mentioned the texts of *Ahadith.* Now it was necessary to give an account of the sources of those *Ahadith* (in terms of their ratings) in the footnotes below, and the references to the printed books should have been stated therein.
3. Whatever unlawful activities and customs Shah Sahib observed around him, he briefly mentioned about them in his book. Those customs and activities had gradually phased out with the passage of time. It was necessary that their characteristic features also be stated briefly so that a reader may I get a clear-cut idea that practicing those things are unlawful indeed. This would help them avoid the other similar activities I which assume different forms and shapes during different periods.
4. During the times of Shah Shaheed, the mode of punctuation in writing was different especially the full stops and comas etc. were not at all observed. Later, the writing system gradually kept developing and advancing. It was necessary that the old style of writing be replaced by the new one by introducing full stops and comas etc. in the text so that the

same becomes easily understandable to the readers, as this step would have enhanced the utility of this book considerably.
5. As it has earlier been mentioned, that even today *Taqwiyat-ul-1man* is a rare book in terms of it's simplicity, comprehensibility, impeccability of text and fascination. Despite all the above facts, some of its words and phrases were not very clearly comprehensible to the readers and therefore required an explanation.

It is not very heartening to note that none of the above could have been accomplished. Some people did pay attention to it, but could not accomplish these tasks according to what was actually required of them. Therefore, a systematic and organized version of *Taqwiyat-ul-1man* is published for the realization and fulfillment of the said purposes.

The present age:

Today, the scope of this book's potential fruitfulness has widened immensely. Instead of being branded as a flag-bearer of *Wahabism* in the common parlance, he is today recognized as a proponent of the great Islamic revival, who raised a banner of *Jihad* (an armed struggle for holy purpose) on the vast land of the Indian subcontinent to lay the foundation of a just and rightful Islamic government. It was a time when all the traces of a thousand years of Muslim domination of the subcontinent were on the wane. He took up the cudgels for purification and independence in an atmosphere which was charged with desolation and dejection. He demonstrated to the Muslims the path of determination, courage and perseverance while the glory of their conquest and dominance was almost breathing its last.

Today, a description of the saga, highlighting his gallant and heroic deeds in his capacity as a *Mujahid* (the one who struggles in the path of Allah) is considered to be as an extremely effective means of imparting a correct religious education, and therefore, it is a tremendous service to render *Taqwiyat-ul-1man* more attractive and worth reading for a Joe-public. This is also an undeniable reality that whatever pronouncements Shah Shaheed had made a hundred and thirty years ago, could not be thoroughly understood and appreciated in terms of its importance and qualitative superiority in all the previous ages as much as it could be realized and appreciated during the present time of ours.

The orderly arrangement of *Taqwiyat-ul-Iman:*

Prior to arranging *Taqwiyat-ul-1man* in an orderly shape, Shah Shaheed had compiled *Ahadith* in the confirmation of *Tauhid* (Oneness of Allah) and the rejection of *Shirk* (associating partners to Allah) and *Bid'at* (inventing new things in religion), a collection which he named *Radd-ul-Ashrak* (in rejection of polytheism). The late Nawab Siddique Hasan Khan had worked on the references and sources of these *Ahadith* and got this collection published under the title of *Al-Idrak li-takhreej Ahadith Radd-ul-Ashrak"* (Perception to infer *Ahadith* in the negation of polytheism). Shah Shaheed only rendered the first portion of this collection into Urdu and this very portion is known as *Taqwiyat-ul-1man*. The remainder of the portion was published by the Late Moulvi Sultan Muhammad in Urdu under the title of *Tadhkir-ul-1khwan* (Reminding to the brothers).

We can not say with any degree of certitude as to in which period *Taqwiyat-ul-Iman* has actually been written. At one place, this book comprises a description of the sanctified Ka'bah's courtyard in such an effective manner that it gives an impression that Shah Shaheed was himself an eye-witness to this spectacle and hence we can deduce that this book must have been written after his return from *Hajj*. Spurred on by the instigation of some of his friends, Mulla Sahib Baghdadi voiced some of his objections on *Taqwiyat-ul-Iman*. Shah Shaheed wrote a letter from Kanpur in response to his objections and the year which is inscribed on this letter is 1240H, which further subscribes to the notion that the said book must have been written in the beginning of 1240H after his return from *Hajj*. During that period, Shah Shaheed had dedicated himself to the task of propagating Islam and organizing for *Jihad* with all his heart and soul and he departed for the cause of *Jihad* on the 7th of Jumada-al-Ukhra 1241H. Upon having read the letter of Shah Shaheed, Mulla Sahib Baghdadi confessed his mistake. Among the scholars of Delhi, the one who was renowned to be the most prominently active in his opposition, was Maulana Fadl Haq Khairabadi, about whom it has been generally acknowledged now that despite having been a dignified scholar and possessing an immense amount of knowledge, his dogmatic precepts and beliefs were no different than that of a Joe-public. He triggered the controversy of the possibility of existence and non-existence of the Prophet's {Peace be upon Him} counterpart and did not take into account the difference between Allah's Will and His Capability to bring something into existence. Shah Shaheed, through his treatise known as *Yak-Rozi* (One-dayer), had proved the baselessness of all these objections. We cannot elaborate on these dimensions here due to the lack of space.

Different versions of *Taqwiyat-ul-Iman:*

The first and foremost task in regard to getting the book rearranged and making it more polished was to collect such versions which are more authentic and have more room for dependability. The versions which were readily available for reference are as follows:
A hand-written version dated 7th of Dhil-Qa'dah 1252H (13th February 1837G) comprising a total of 114 pages, each page consisting of 14 lines, and each line containing 16 words. This is the oldest manuscript available in the humble view of the writer. Some of its pages are rather moth-eaten. The first eight pages are not available.
1. A hand-written version comprising 237 pages, each page consisting of 8 lines, each line comprising 14 words, excellent handwriting and a fine paper. Date of writing has not been mentioned on it.
2. A printed version of *Taqwiyat-ul-Iman* published by Darul-Uloom Printing press, Delhi in the year 1847 G, containing altogether 92 pages. It has not been confirmed as to what edition it exactly was, as no other copy of its former printed version is available to us.
3. A copy of its type-written version (cursive style). This version was corrected by Moulana Muhammad Hasan under the auspices of Moulvi Abdul-Latif and Moulvi Kamil under the supervision of Munshi Ghulam Maula and Munshi Wajid Sahib and was printed in Muhsini Printing Press, Calcutta. The printing was completed in 1854 G. A special attention was paid to the correction of the text in the said version. A comparison of the texts reveals that the reviser has effected a few changes in it. In addition to this one, we also had an opportunity to refer to several other editions as well. An edition which was published by *Jamiyat-ud-Da'wath   Wat-Tabligh* (Association for the propagation of Islam) and compiled by Maulana Muhiuddin Ahmad Qusuri is especially worth-mentioning.

The principles of getting it organized:

We have had some detailed discussions with some dignified and accomplished scholars in regard to determining the regulations and limits of getting this book re-organized and render it more refined and polished. All those scholars were bona fide ones and were really worth giving their views about it. Some observed that all the archaic words and obsolete idiomatic phrases should be changed accordingly and some complexities in the syntax should be altered necessarily at least to such an extent that it should be easily comprehensible to the ones who are only accustomed to studying the books written in the present-day prose style. These kinds of partial changes had been effected earlier also, but pursuant to giving this matter a profound thought, it seemed suitable that no part of it be modified and the text should be printed in its original form as it was, after purging it from imperfections through a laborious research. However, the style of punctuation which was prevalent during the times of Shah Shaheed was avoided and the present style of punctuation was adopted. For instance:

1. During Shah Shaheed's times, some of the words were written in a spliced form. But in the recent version, these words have been printed separately according to the present day practice.
2. Some verbal forms denoting tenses, which had different grammatical shapes during the times of Shah Shaheed, have been changed according to the present day usage in the new version.
3. The whole book has been covered with the punctuation marks so that the sentences and phrases become clearly distinguishable. The words like 'and' etc. which were then being used as a comma or a dash, have also been deleted in the new edition. According to our view, none of the above may be considered a change in the main text as this is only a difference in the mode of punctuation.
4. The words and phrases that required an interpretation have been explained either in the footnotes below, or a word or two have been added in the main text within parenthesis (brackets).
5. Those *Ahadith* which were partially referred to in the main text, have been completed in the footnotes.
6. Shah Shaheed, while referring to the translation of some of the Qur'anic verses, only focused on its implied meanings and the message he intended to convey through it. In regard to the literal translation of such verses, the translation of Shah Abdul-Qadir Muhaddith {May Allah have mercy on him} has been presented in the book.

The last word:

Within the limits of one resources and capabilities, we have tried our utmost to make the reading of this book more and more easy, attractive and enjoyable. What ever amount of success we have achieved in this regard so far, we only think of it as a miracle of the ever present mercy and blessing of Allah the Exalted. In case this meager endeavor of ours does happen to contain some flaws, we consider it to be a shortcoming of our mind and perception and hence, owe our apologies to our dear readers.

We, however, should hasten to add that the only purpose we had in our minds was to broaden the scope of the profitability of this important religious accomplishment of Shah Shaheed to its maximum length so that the Muslims may become Muslims in the true sense of the word.

And last but not least, our ultimate supplication is that the praise is to Allah, the Cherisher and

Sustainer of the worlds, and our salutations and greetings to the Lord of all the Messengers.

Ghulam Rasool Mehr

PRELUDE

Eulogies and Glorifications:

Oh our Lord! It is incumbent upon us to express our thanks and gratitude to You that You have bestowed on us Your endless bounties and favors and blessed us with Your guidance to the only true religion (untainted and authentic faith enjoying the privilege of Your concurrence). You have led us to the right path of Islamic Monotheism, made us one of the followers of the Prophet of Islam {Peace be upon Him}a , blessed us with an ardent favor to learn religion and have kindled a feeling of affection within our hearts for the people who observe religious norms in their day to-day lives. Oh our Lord! We beseech You to shower Your blessings and mercy on Your beloved Messenger {Peace be upon Him}, his family and progeny, his Companions and his successors. We entreat you to include us too among them and give us strength to lead an Islamic way of life. Please make our ending on Islam and include our names within the list of Your obedient slaves. *Amin.* (O Allah accept it)

Servant and servitude:

All the human beings are the slaves of Allah. The duty of a slave is to carry out instructions given to him and the one who shirks his responsibility is not a slave. The slavery or servitude is based on the correctness of Faith. The one whose Faith has deficiency, his service is regarded as unacceptable and whosoever is blessed with the correctness of Faith, even a small fraction of his service thus rendered is deemed creditable. Hence, it is an obligation on every Muslim to strive to maintain his Faith (according to the exacting standards of Islamic Monotheism). Furthermore, one should accord the foremost preference to matters concerning the rectification of his Faith over the rest of the matters in his day-to-day life.

The prevalent conditions:

The present day situation is that the people have adopted different ways. Some of them pursue the traditions cherished by their forefathers, some swear by the methodologies devised by the saints, some proffer the self-proclaimed observations of the scholars as evidence whereas some merely run their own conjectures and poke their nose into the matters of religion on the pretext of using their intellect.

The best choice:

The best possible option is that we should regard Qur'an and *Sunnah* as a yardstick of excellence, refrain from interfering into the matters concerning the Islamic law by applying our intellect into it and must slake the thirst of our soul by resorting to these two affluents (i.e. Qur'an and *Sunnah*). We must recognize the sayings of the saints, observations of the scholars and the customs observed within one's community in case the said things confirm to the standards set forth by Qur'an and *Sunnah* and likewise we should rejectfully shun them in case they do not.

It is not an uphill task to understand religion:

A myth which has gained much currency among the masses is that to have an understanding of Qur'an and *Hadith* is a difficult task for it requires a lot of knowledge and as long as we are ignorant, we can neither understand it nor we could act upon it. Only the saints and pious people possess the capability to act accordingly. This notion which is nursed by them is absolutely baseless because Allah the Exalted has stated that the verses of the Noble Qur'an are explicit and conspicuously clear as mentioned in the following verse:

{And indeed We have sent down to you manifest *Ayat* (verses) and none disbelieve in them but the *Fasiqun* (those who rebel against Allah's Command).}(V.2:99)

The above statement means that it is not difficult to understand them at all but it is difficult to act upon them as their compliance seems to be fairly hard on one's self and therefore the disobedient ones do not recognize them.

Why were the Messengers sent?

It does not require a lot of knowledge to have an understanding of Qur'an and *Sunnah* as the Messengers were sent to provide guidance and directions to the ignorant and the illiterates and to impart knowledge to the unlearned people as stated in one of the verses of the Noble Qur'an:

{He it is Who sent among the unlettered ones a Messenger from among themselves, reciting to them His verses, purifying them and teaching them the Book and *Al-Hikmah* (legal ways). And verily, they had been before in manfest error.}(V.62:2)

This is one of the great bounties of Allah that He deputed such a Prophet who taught the unlearned, purified the impure, imparted knowledge to the ignorant, wisdom to the unwise and guidance to the delinquent. Even after grasping the import of this verse, if some one still insists that it is the job of the learned to comprehend Qur'an, and the great saints to act upon it's teachings, it only tantamount to rejecting the above noted Qur'anic verse and depreciating this grand bounty of Allah. The fact is that by acquiring an understanding of the above, the ignorant persons become the learned ones and the delinquent ones turn into scholars by acting upon the teachings transcribed therein.

An instance of a physician and a sick person:

To elaborate it hypothetically, let us assume that on one hand we have an expert and wise physician, while on another hand, we have another person who is suffering from some kind of a horrendous ailment. By way of sympathy, a third person advises him to consult such and such physician for his treatment, but this sick person observes that to approach this physician, and get treated by him is the task of those who are hale and hearty and as long as I am mortally sick, how could I possibly go to him for treatment? Won't you think of this person to be mentally decrepit as he does not recognize the efficacy of a doctor's treatment. A physician is meant to provide treatment to the invalids. Does a person deserve to be called a doctor who claims to provide treatment only to the hale and hearty? Thus we may reasonably conclude that an ignorant and delinquent person equally needs to understand Qur'an and *Hadith* and act upon it fervently as does a saint and a scholarly person. It is an obligation on all and sundry to continue their pursuit of the knowledge concerning the teachings of Qur'an and *Sunnah,* put their heart and soul into understanding it, act upon it accordingly and mould their Faith within it's framework..

Monotheism and prophethood:

We must remember that *lman* (Faith) has two constituents:

a) To consider Allah as the only One, worthy of being worshipped.

b) To recognize the prophethood of Messengers of Allah.

To consider Allah as the only One, worthy of being worshipped, means that we should not associate partners with Him and to recognize the prophethood of the Messenger implies that we must follow him and act according to his instructions. The first constituent of Faith is to *conform* to the Islamic Monotheism and the second one is to comply with *Sunnah* (teachings of the Prophet {Peace be upon Him}.The opposite of Monotheism is polytheism and the antonym of *Sunnah* is *Bid'ah* (innovation). It is obligatory on every Muslim to strictly adhere to the concept of Islamic Monotheism and to comply with the teachings of the Prophet {Peace be upon Him}.One must abide by them and avoid slipping into the acts of *Shirk* (polytheism; i.e. associating partners with Allah) or *Bid'ah* (innovating new things in religion). *Shirk* and *Bid'ah* may be considered as a termite that eats into the sinews of Faith and destroys it. As far as other vices are concerned, their commission only impedes the process of pursuing pious deeds. Therefore, a person who is characterized by the qualities of being a monotheist, follower of *Sunnah,* averse to *Shirk* and *Bid'a* and whose accompaniment inspires an inclination towards compliance of *Sunnah,* is indeed a person who should be taken as a religious instructor and mentor.

On this treatise *Taqwiyat-ul-Iman:*

In this book entitled *Taqwiyat-ul lman,* we have compiled a few Qur'anic verses and *Ahddith* which elaborate the Oneness of Allah, compliance with *Sunnah,* and the vices of *Shirk* and *Bid'ah.* This has been translated into simple English along with short footnotes for the purpose of giving explanations so that everybody can benefit from it and whomsoever Allah wills, may be led to the Right Path. May Allah accept it as a means of our deliverance in the Hereafter. *Amin.* It has been named *Taqwiyatul-Iman* which comprises two chapters. The first chapter consists of description concerning the concept of Islamic Monotheism and the wickedness of polytheism and the second chapter consists of compliance with *Sunnah* and the vices of *Bid'ah.*

Chapter One
Description of *Tauhid*

People's unawareness and ignorance:

Polytheism is generally widespread among the people and the concept of Monotheism is in scarcity. Many people who claim to be the bearers of Faith do not understand the meanings of *Tauhid* and *Shirk* (Monotheism and polytheism). Apparently they are Muslims, but they are unconsciously involved in the acts of *Shirk*. Therefore, first we should try to understand the meanings of *Tauhid* (Monotheism) and *Shirk* (polytheism) so that we may know about their advantages and disadvantages as directed by Qur'an and *Sunnah*.

The acts leading to polytheism:

In difficult times and situations people call upon saints, Prophets, *Imam,* martyrs, angels and fairies for assistance; make their vows to them, invoke them for the fulfillment of their wishes and even make so-called offerings to them so that their wishes may come true. To avoid ailments, they have no scruples about attributing their sons to those false deities by giving them such names as Abdun-Nabi, Ali Bakhsh, Hussain Bakhsh, Peer Bakhsh, Madar Bakhsh, Salar Bakhsh, Ghulam Muhiuddin and Ghulam Moinuddin etc. Someone raises a plait of hair in the name of a deity, someone slaughters an animal in their names, someone invokes them in a distressed situation and someone swears an oath in their names. This means that the way non-Muslims treat their gods and goddesses, these so-called Muslims also give exactly a similar treatment to the Prophets, saints, *Imam,* martyrs, angels and fairies. Despite committing all the above sinful acts, they still claim to be Muslims. As Allah has rightfully said:

{And most of them believe not in Allah except that they attribute partners unto Him.} (V.12:106)

Those who profess to have Faith in Allah while their actions reeking of polytheism:

It means that the majority of people who outwardly profess to have faith in Allah are in fact entangled in the quagmire of polytheism. If someone questions them as to why are they involved in *Shirk* while evincing faith in Allah, they answer by saying that we are not committing an act of polytheism, neigh we cherish a tremendous amount of love for the prophets and saints and we are none but their true devotees. Had we considered them on an equal status with Allah, it would have been 'an act of *Shirk',* but we merely consider them the slaves and creatures of Allah, Who had vested in them an authority and given them the capability to the effect that they manipulate the matters concerning this world by the Will of Allah. Therefore calling upon them for help is calling upon Allah for His Help. These people are dear ones to Allah and therefore are free to do whatever they like. These are our advocates who will intercede with Allah on our behalf. Meeting them makes one meet his Cherisher and calling upon them makes us near to Allah. The more we recognize their greatness and pay our respect to them, the more we shall be drawn towards Allah. In addition to all this, they make a lot of other absurd and baseless statements.

The verdict of Qur'an:

The sole reason for all the above incongruities is that people have forsaken Qur'an and *Hadith* and exercise their own judgments in the matters concerning *Shari 'ah* by applying their own intellect, pursue myths and superstitions, and try to justify their erroneous customs and traditions by presenting insubstantial evidence. If they had the knowledge of Qur'an and *Hadith,* they would have known that even the pagans among the Arabs used to employ similar kind of arguments before the Prophet {Peace be upon Him}.Allah's wrath befell them as He declared them liars in one of the Qur'anic verses:

> {And they worship besides Allah things that hurt them not, nor profit them, and they say: 'These are our intercessors with Allah.' Say: Do you inform Allah of that which He knows not in the heavens and on the earth? Glorified and Exalted is He above all that which they associate as partners with Him!} (V.l0:18)

None but Allah is the Capable:

The objects which the polytheists offer their worship to, are absolutely powerless. They possess no capability of either benefiting anybody or inflicting any harm on someone. As to their notion that they will intercede with Allah on their behalf, is nothing but a mere fallacy for the simple reason that Allah did not inform them about any such thing. Do they profess to be more knowledgeable than Allah in regard to the matters of this world and the heavens in what they believe to be their mediators with Allah on their behalf? 'Thus, it becomes known to us that there is no such mediator in this universe who, on the basis of people's belief or disbelief in them, can either benefit or harm someone. Even the intercession of the Prophets and saints itself is governed by Allah. Nothing happens if someone calls upon them in distress. Furthermore, we are warned that whoever ,worships someone as his intercessor, is also a *'Mushrik'* as stated by Allah in this verse:

> {And those who take *Auliya* (protectors and helpers) besides Him (say): 'We worship them only that they may bring us near to Allah.' Verily, Allah will judge between them concerning that wherein they differ. Truly, Allah guides not him who is a liar, and a disbeliever.} (V.39:3)

None is the supporter other than Allah:

The fact is that Allah is very close to a human being but the human beings themselves got distracted from this basic truth and coined a fallacious concept believing that an idol shall draw us near Allah and thus took such idols to be their mediators. These are the people who shamelessly turned down the bounty of Allah that it is He who listens to everyone directly and fulfills everyone's desires. Instead of turning to Allah, they started directing their prayers and invocations towards the so-called deities other than Allah for the fulfillment of their wishes. To make the matters worse, these people also wished to, be near to Allah by employing erroneous and wrong methods. How could these ingrates and untruthful people be guided on the Right Path? The more they tread on this crooked path, the more shall they be driven away from the Right Path.

None is the sustainer other than Allah:

This clarifies that whosoever worships the so called deities in the hope that worshipping them shall make him nearer to Allah, is none but a polytheist, an accomplished liar and the one who rejects the bounty of Allah. Allah states in one of the Qur'anic verses:

{Say: In Whose Hand is the sovereignty of everything (i.e. treasures of each and everything)? And He protects (all), while against Whom there is no protector, (i.e. if Allah saves anyone none can punish or harm him, and if Allah punishes or harms anyone none can save him), if you know. They will say: '(All that belongs) to Allah.' Say: 'How then are you deceived and turn away from the truth?'} (V.23:88-89)

Even if the polytheists are asked about an entity who exercises an absolute control over the whole universe and against whom no one can stand, they will definitely say it is Allah. When Allah is All-Powerful, is not it an act of lunacy to associate partners with Allah? Thus it becomes known to us that Allah has not given anyone authority to dispose off universal matters and no one is either capable of supporting someone else. Furthermore, even the polytheists of the prophetic era did not consider the idols to be on a par with Allah in terms of status, but considered them as slaves and creatures of Allah. They also knew that these idols did not possess any of the Divine powers, but their *Shirk* was represented by calling upon them, making vows to them, presenting offerings to them and considering them as their intercessors with Allah. This means that whosoever accords someone a similar treatment, even though by reckoning him to be a slave and a creature, such a person is bound to be regarded as a counterpart of Abu Jahl in terms of polytheism.

The reality of *Shirk* (Polytheism):

Shirk does not only imply that an entity be equated with Allah or be reckoned as His counterpart, but it goes much further to include the things and manners which Allah has peculiarized to His Qualities and that represent the signs of worshipping and obeisance which He has specified for his slaves to observe for Him Alone. In case, someone observes those signs and exhibits them in front of any other entity whatsoever other than Allah, such a practice also lies within the definition of *Shirk:* this practice includes making prostrations, sacrificing an animal in the Name of Allah, making vows, calling upon Him in distress, considering Allah to be Himself present everywhere, and maintaining that the others do have a role to play in the matters of one's fate and destiny. All the above are different shapes and varieties of *Shirk.* Prostration is particularized to be performed for the sake of Allah only, animal sacrifice is done for Him Alone, vows are made to Him Alone, He is the One, Who, in times of distress (situations), is called upon. He is the Omnipotent and All-Powerful and He is the Supreme Authority over everything. If any of these qualities are ascribed to any other entity other than Allah, it is known as *Shirk,* even if such an entity is regarded as inferior to Allah or is reckoned to be a creature or slave of Allah.

All such beings and entities like a Prophet, saint, jinn, Satan, ghost, apparition and fairy shall all be treated equally in this matter and whoever considers them as having Divine powers commits an act of *Shirk* and the doer of such a thing will become a *Mushrik* (the one who associates partners with Allah). Hence Allah has brought down His wrath on the Jews and Christians too even though they did not practice idolatry, but treated their Prophets and saints in a similar manner (i.e. they attributed to them the qualities which are purely Divine in nature) as Allah has stated in the following Qur'anic verse:

{They (Jews and Christians) took their rabbis and their monks to be their lords besides Allah, (by obeying them in things which they made lawful or unlawful according to their own desires without being ordered by Allah) and (they also took as their lord) Messiah, son of Mary, while they (Jews and Christians) were commanded (in the Torah and the Gospel) to worship none but One (God-Allah) *La ilaha ilia Huwa* (none has the right to be worshipped but He). Praise and glory is to Him, (far above is He) from having the partners they associate (with Him).}(V.9:31)

It means that even though they considered Allah as the Most Supreme Lord, but besides that, they also gave their recognition to other mini-lords, which are their priests and monks. These people were never instructed to commit such acts of *Shirk*. Allah is all Alone worthy of being worshipped. He has no partners. Everyone, whether big or small, are none but His helpless slaves.

Allah states in one of the verses of the Noble Qur'an:

{There is none in the heavens and the earth but comes unto the Most Beneficent (Allah) as a slave. Verily, He knows each one of them, and has counted them a full counting. And everyone of them will come to Him alone on the Day of Resurrection (without any helper, or protector or defender,)}. (V.19:93-95)

It means that regardless whether a creature happens to be an angel or a human being, it carries a status of no more than being a slave before Allah. A slave lies under an absolute hegemony of Allah and therefore, is completely helpless and powerless. Everything lies under Allah's control. He gives nobody under anyone's control. Everyone shall have to appear in His Presence to account for his deeds. No one will advocate for anyone there nor one could lend his support to anyone else. There are hundreds of verses mentioned in this regard in the Noble Qur'an whereas only we, as a specimen, have made a mention of a few of them. Whosoever understands them clearly, shall have a clear understanding of the concept of *Shirk* and *Tauhid*. *In sha 'Allah*.

Chapter Two
Categories and aspects of *Shirk* (Polytheism)

It is necessary to gain knowledge about the characteristics which Allah has peculiarised for Himself so that none of them be attributed to any other else. Such things are countless. We, on our part, shall be mentioning some of those things and prove them in the background of Qur'an and *Hadith* so that the people may understand the other pertinent things also with their help.

1. *Shirk* in knowledge:

The first thing is that Allah is present everywhere by His Knowledge which means that His Knowledge encompasses everything. This is why He has a complete cognizance of everything, every time, whether a thing happens to be far or near, hidden or apparent, up in the heavens or inside the earth, on the tops of the mountains or at the bottom of an ocean. This magnificence belongs to none but Allah. If a person calls upon someone (by invoking his name) other than Allah, while doing his everyday routine chores, so that the one called upon may help him obviate his distress, or attacks an enemy by invoking his name, or keeps pronouncing his name on the beads of a rosary, or makes a vow in his name or conjures up his picture in his imagination by nursing a faith that whenever he invokes his name, or think of him vividly in his mind or contemplate on his grave, he gains cognizance of him; none of his affairs is hidden from him, and whatever circumstances he goes through, namely, sickness and good health, abundance and distress, life and death, sadness and happiness etc., are all known to him; any word which his mouth utters is heard by him and he knows about his thoughts and imaginations. All the above things and acts prove the presence of the elements of *Shirk*. This is called a *Shirk* in knowledge which means one is trying to prove that someone other than Allah possesses a similar kind of knowledge which is only the prerogative of Allah.

By nursing this kind of faith, a man undoubtedly turns into a *Mushrik* (polytheist) whether he nurses such a faith in regard to an honorable human being or any of the exalted angels, or whether such a knowledge which is attributed to him, happens to be a personal one or granted by Allah. Whatever the situation may be, this is an absolutely polytheistic faith.

2. *Shirk* in disposing:

Disposing the matters of the universe with intention, exercising authority, killing at will and resuscitating, awarding abundance and giving distress, giving healthiness and sickness, giving victory and defeat, succeeding and preceding, fulfillment of one's desires, obviating calamities, providing help in distress situations and whenever one stands in need of it, are all attributed to Allah and none but Him Alone. None but Allah can have this magnificence. A human being or an angel, despite acquiring great ranks, may never have these characteristics. A person who seeks to prove that an entity other than Allah may have an authority of this nature, makes vows to this entity or makes an animal sacrifice for the purpose of fulfillment of his wishes, and invokes it's name in distress so that it can obviate his troubles, such a person is called *'Mushrik'* and this kind of act is called '*Shirk* in authority' or disposing. It means that cherishing a belief that any entity other than Allah may have this authority, whether as the one granted by Allah or as one of it's personal traits, is a polytheistic faith anyway.

3. *Shirk* in worship:

Allah has particularised all acts of worship for Him Alone which are defined as *Ibadat* like prostrating, bowing, standing with folded hands, giving charity in the Name of Allah, fasting in His Name and undertaking long journeys to visit His Sacred House by putting on such a clothing that the people may distinguish them as the visitors of His Sanctified House, invoking Allah's Name on the way, avoiding indecent talk and hunting, circumambulating His House with an utmost caution, making prostrations in its direction, carrying the animals of sacrifice towards it, making vows there, putting a covering on Ka'bah, making supplications while standing on the threshold of Ka'bah, asking for the virtuosities in the religious as well as worldly matters, kissing of the Black-Stone, touching the walls of Ka'bah by one's mouth and chest, making supplications by getting hold of the fringes of its covering, illuminating its surroundings, taking up residence there as one of its servants, sweeping and cleaning it, offer drinking water to the pilgrims, providing water for *Wudu* (ablution) and bathing, partaking of *Zamzam* water by considering it as a sanctified act, getting oneself drenched with it, drinking it to one's heart content, distributing it among themselves, carrying it to be presented to one's relatives, venerating the forest surrounding it, to refrain from hunting there, not to cut trees there, not to pullout grass from there, not to graze animals there: these are acts which Allah has prescribed for Muslims to be observed as His worship.

Now, if a person makes a bow or prostration before the grave of a Prophet, saint, ghost, apparition, jinn, fairy or any of the real or fake graves or a specified place inside a tomb, or a certain sign or house, or a Eucharist and coffin; observes fast in their names; stands in front of them with folded hands; makes offerings to them or hoisting a flag in their name or walking backwards (with a reverse motion of feet); kisses a grave or undertakes a long journey to visit graves and other places; lights earthen lamps there or makes arrangements for illuminating them; or puts coverings on their walls or offers a sheet as a covering on the grave, manually fanning the air by hand (by using a Morchhal, a fanning contrivance); erects a tent there; kisses it's threshold; offers supplications there with folded hands; asks for the fulfillment of wishes there; serves the shrine by becoming its servant and venerates the forest around it: anyone doing any of the above acts commits a clear and manifest *Shirk*.

In brief, all the above acts and the alike, are called "*Shirk* in worship." It implies paying one's respect to an entity other than Allah in a manner which is prescribed for Allah Alone either by believing that this particular entity is personally entitled to such a veneration or by believing that Allah becomes pleased if any of these entities are held in high esteem or with the blessing of their veneration, troubles are warded off and done away with. Whatever may be the case, such faith is purely polytheistic in its nature.

4. *Shirk* in one's daily routine chores:

Allah the Exalted has taught His slaves the norms of respect to the effect that they should remember Allah while performing their everyday worldly chores and pay Him their tributes for the enhancement of their Faith and to secure Allah's blessing in day-to-day assignments. These norms include: (1) making vows to Allah and calling upon Him Alone whenever a catastrophe befalls his slave; (2) invoking His Name for His blessing whenever commencing an assignment; (3) slaughtering animals to express one's gratitude to Allah in the case of having been blessed with a child; (4) giving one's children such names as Abdullah, Abdur-Rahman, Ilahi Bakhsh, Allah Diya, Amatullah, Allah Di etc.; (5) taking out a small portion of the crop produce and giving it away in the Name of Allah; (6) apportioning some of the fruits to His name out of the total produce; (7) specifying some of the animals and allocating them for the purpose of sacrifice in the Name of Allah; (8) treating the animals which are carried to the House of Allah with due respect by neither riding them nor mounting any load on them; (9) observing Divine Instructions in the manners concerning food and dress; (10) restricting oneself to the use of permissible things only and avoiding the ones that are not allowed; (11) considering that all the different conditions and situations which one comes across in this world, like expensive and inexpensive rates and prices, health and sickness, victory and defeat, succeeding and preceding, sadness and happiness, are all commanded by Allah; (12) pronouncing a standard formula of *In Sha' Allah* while making an intention to perform an assignment; (13) pronouncing the Name of Allah the Exalted One in such a manner that His Greatness is conspicuously highlighted and one's slavery is clearly exhibited, by using such words like, our *Rubb,* our Master, our Creator *or Ma'bud* (the object of our worship) etc.; (14) in case a need arises on a certain occasion to administer an oath at all, undertaking an oath only in the Name of Allah.

These and the other similar things have been singled out by Allah as His own and personal prerogative for the sake of His veneration and magnificence. Anybody showing such kind of respect to an entity other than Allah, commits *Shirk;* as for example: making a vow to it with the intention of facilitating a difficult assignment; giving one's children names like AbdunNabi, Imam Bakhsh, Peer Bakhsh etc.; apportioning part of the produce of one's farm or orchard to it's name; separating part of the fruits and keeping them aside (in the name of a deity) immediately after they are picked up from trees and then only putting the rest to, one's use; dedicating some animals from among the whole herd to a deity and then treating those animals with respect by not removing them from the fodder and water and not to strike them with stick or stone; observing customs and traditions in terms of dress and food to the effect that a specified group of people should not eat such and such food and should not wear such and such dress; attributing the virtues and evils of the world to them by making such statements that as long as that particular person has been cursed by that particular deity, he has gone mad or that certain person has turned into a handicapped person due to the fact that he was driven away by that deity or by saying that as long as that person was blessed by a certain saint, he is now on a flood tide of success; or that famine was wrought by that star or by observing that this assignment was not accomplished as long as the same was commenced at a certain time and on a certain date or by observing that if Allah and His Prophet will it, one would be coming; or by saying that it will happen if one's religious mentor wishes it to take place or using such adjectives like, the Sustainer, Independent, Lord of lords, the Master of the universe or the King of kings etc.; the undertaking of an oath in the name of the Prophet or the Qur'an or Ali {May Allah have mercy on him}or an *Imam,* or a religious mentor or their graves or one's own self etc.

All the above practices generate *Shirk* which is called a *'Shirk* in day-to-day chores', which implies paying one's respect to an entity other than Allah exactly in the same manner as the one prescribed for Allah.

These four kinds of *Shirk* have been clearly stated in the Qur'an and *Hadith* and therefore we shall be mentioning about them in the next chapters.

Chapter Three
The Vices of Polytheism---
The Virtues of Monotheism

The polytheism cannot be forgiven:

{Verily! Allah forgives not (the sin of) setting up partners in worship with Him, but He forgives whom He pleases, sins other than that, and whoever sets up partners in worship with Allah, has indeed strayed far away.}(V.4:116)

The one who does not discriminate between the permissible and the forbidden, commits theft, idles away his time doing nothing, shuns his prayers and fasting, does not give his wife and children their due rights and becomes incumbent on disobeying his parents -has indeed strayed from the path of Allah, but the one who gets strangled in the quagmire of *Shirk* has strayed very much far away by getting involved in such a sinful act as shall never be forgiven by Allah except by showing repentance. As far as other sins are concerned, Allah may perhaps forgive them even without repentance (on the part of the slave). It becomes thus known that *Shirk* is an unpardonable crime and the person who commits it is bound to be punished. If an act of *Shirk*, thus committed, is of such an extreme kind which turns a person into a polytheist, then the penalty thus incurred by the person is an eternal Hell-fire, for he will neither be ever released from it, nor shall get any rest and peace whatsoever therein. As to the acts of minor degree of *Shirk*[1], their doers are bound to be penalized according to the penalties which are apportioned for them by Allah the Exalted.

As far as the penalties which have been specified by Allah in regard to other sinful acts are concerned, they mainly depend on the Will of Allah. (Depending on His Will, He may forgive them or, He may punish the doer).

Explaining *Shirk*:

We thus understand that *Shirk* is the biggest of all sins (i.e. and no sin surpasses it in terms of gravity, severity and enormity). It can be explained by the following example:

Let us suppose that a king has a specific penal code for his subjects comprising all kinds of penalties for different kinds of offences like, theft, robbery, sleeping while being on duty as a guard, a delayed arrival at the king's court, fleeing from the battlefield and delaying the payment of government revenues etc. are all crimes deserving specific punishments. The king, depending on his will, can either duly punish the offenders or forgive them, but there are a few crimes whose commission clearly indicates a rebellion, like an act of coronating and enthroning a nobleman, a

---

[1] Whether a *'Shirk'* is of a monstrous nature or of a minor degree, is forbidden anyway and is contrary to the concept of Islamic Monotheism.

minister, a fief, a chieftain, a sweeper or a shoe-maker and declaring anyone of the above as a king in the presence of the king himself. Such an act shall be considered as a mutiny. Or similarly, if a throne or a crown is made for any of the above categories of people or anyone of them is called with such title as 'Your Excellency' or 'His Highness' or 'His Majesty' or is treated with the observance of a royal protocol or a certain day is specified for him as a gala festival or a certain vow is made to him after a royal fashion, is what constitutes the greatest of all crimes which must never go unpunished. A monarch who overlooks giving out punishments on such crimes, is bound to have a weak and staggering empire and the wise people shall libel such a monarch as incapable and unworthy of ruling an empire. Dear friends! Let us fear from the Master of the universe, the Sovereign who has a great sense of honor and an unlimited power. How can such a Lord let the polytheists go unpunished! May Allah bless all the Muslims with His mercy and save them from such dangerous calamities as *Shirk. Amin!*

Shirk, the greatest of all vices:

Allah the Exalted One says in one of His verses:

{And (remember) when Luqman said to his son when he was advising him: *'Join* not in worship others with Allah. Verily! Joining others in worship with Allah is a great *Zulm* (wrong) indeed.}(V.3l:13)

It means that Allah had awarded clairvoyance to Luqman {May Allah have mercy on him} By utilizing his mental faculties, he understood that giving away someone's right to someone else is an act of great injustice. The one who gives away Allah's Right to someone else among His creatures is similar to a person who gives away something to the meanest one, what in fact is due to be given to the greatest one. As long as Allah is the Greatest of all and all His creatures rank no more than a slave before Him, what injustice should be greater than putting a royal crown on the head of a shoe-maker! We must understand that anyone whether one of the most eminent human beings or any of the angels dearest and nearest to Allah does not carry the status of even a shoe-maker in terms of frivolity and disgrace, while facing the magnificence of Divinity. Thus it becomes clear that as *Shari'ah* has regarded *Shirk* to be an extremely enormous sinful act, one's wisdom and common intellect also recognizes *Shirk* to be as such. It is the greatest of all vices which is a fact, because the greatest of all inequities to be found in a man is that he should disrespect his elders. Who else is bigger than Allah in greatness! Committing an act of *Shirk* verily amounts to being disrespectful towards Him.

Tauhid (Monotheism) is the only way out:

Allah has said in one of the verses of the Noble Qur'an:

{And we did not send any Messenger before you *(O* Muhammad {peace be upon Him}*)* but We inspired him (saying): La *ilaha illa Ana* [none has the right to be worshipped but I (Allah)], so worship Me (Alone and none else).} (V.2l:25)

It means that all the Messengers were sent by Allah with exactly the same commandment that none but Allah should be worshipped and only Allah is worthy of being worshipped. We thus understand that the commandment in regard to the recognition of Oneness of Allah and the prohibition concerning the joining of others in worship with Him is a matter which is a common constituent of all the previous revealed doctrines, and hence this is the only way out for one's salvation. The rest of all the other creeds are in error.

Allah is disgusted with *Shirk*:

It is reported by Abu Hurairah {May Allah have mercy on him} that Allah's Messenger {Peace be upon Him} said: Allah has made the following statement:

> "I am most dispensed with the action of joining others in worship with Me. Whosoever does an act in which he joins others in worship with Me, I shun him and his partners and become disgusted with him."

It means that unlike others who divide their shared goods among themselves, I do not do so because I stand in need of no one. Whoever performs a virtuous deed for Me by giving Me a partner in it, I do not even take My share and leave the whole of it for others and become disgusted with him. It thus becomes known to us that whoever does an act for Allah, and does the same act for an entity other than Allah, he has indeed committed *Shirk* and it further elaborates that any act of worship which is dedicated to Allah by the polytheists is unacceptable. Allah is disgusted with such acts and such people.

Affirming the Oneness of Allah prior to the dawn of time itself:

Allah the Exalted says:

> {And (remember) when your Lord brought forth from the children of Adam, from their loins, their seed (or from Adam's loin his offspring) and made them testify as to themselves (saying): 'Am I not your Lord?' They said: 'Yes! We testify,' lest you should say on the Day of Resurrection: 'Verily, we have been unaware of this. Or lest you should say: 'It was only our fathers aforetime who took others as partners in worship along with Allah, and we were (merely their) descendants after them; will You then destroy us because of the deeds of men who practiced *Al-Batil* (i.e. polytheism and committing crimes and sins, invoking and worshipping others besides Allah)?}(V.7:172,173)

It has been reported by Ahmad on the authority of Ubai bin {May Allah have mercy on him} in regard to the interpretation of the verse (regarding the time when Allah made the offspring of Adam testify) saying that Allah gathered all the progeny of Adam, formed them in pairs, then made their facial features and shapes, then gave them the power of speech. When they began to speak, He took a covenant from them by asking them, "Am I not your *Rabb?*" They answered, "Verily, You are our *Rabb!*"[1] Allah then stated, "I hereby make all the seven strata of heavens

---

[1] *Rabb* means among other things, the Creator, the Sustainer, the Provider and the One in Whose hand is the disposal of all affairs.[I] Thus they confirmed to it. Then Allah elevated Adam (to a certain height) who could see all of them. he saw that there rich among them as well as poor, beautiful as well as ugly. Upon sighting this, Adam enquired of Allah, "O our *Rabb!* Why didn't You create all of them as equals?" He answered, "I like to be offered thanks." Then A dam {Peace be upon Him} sighted among them the Prophets {Peace be upon Them} too whose faces were glowing like lamps and who had an aura of illumination surrounding their faces. Then Allah the Exalted took also an acknowledgement from all the Prophets in regard to their Prophethood. It alludes to that pledge which is mentioned in

and earth as well as your father Adam a witness unto you lest you should employ an excuse of being unaware of it on the Day of Resurrection. Be certain that none is worthy of being worshipped except Me and none but Me is your *Rabb*. Do not associate partners with Me in worshipping. I shall keep sending my Messengers unto you who will in turn continue to remind you of this covenant of yours with Me and I shall reveal my Books unto you." All of them answered, "We hereby testify that You are our *Rabb* and You are the object of our worship. None but You is our Lord and none but You is worthy of our worship.

Shirk cannot be presented as an authority:

Ubai bin Ka'b{May Allah have mercy on him}, while interpreting the above verse said that Allah gathered all the offspring of Adam at one place, formed them into groups, for instance, He separated the Prophets, saints, martyrs, pious people, obedient ones, disobedient ones into different groups. Similarly, He segregated the Jews, the Christians, the polytheists and the followers of every religion. Then whatever facial features and shapes one had to be given in this world, Allah made them appear exactly in the same manner there accordingly. Someone was made to appear as good-looking, someone as bad-looking, someone as conversant, someone as dumb, and someone as a lame person. Then all of them were given the faculty of speech and then asked, "Am I not your *Rabb?"* All of them acknowledged the lordship of Allah and then Allah took a pledge from all of them to the effect that they shall not take anyone as their ruler and master except Him Alone and shall not consider anyone worthy of being worshipped except Him Alone. Then Allah made all the seven strata of heavens and earth as witnesses and said that the Prophets shall be sent unto you to remind you of this pledge of yours and they shall bring with them the heavenly scriptures. Everyone has individually affirmed the Oneness of Allah and rejected associating partners with Him in an era prior to the dawn of time itself and therefore, no one may be presented as an evidence in the matter of *Shirk* (i.e. a preceptor, a mendicant, a sheikh, a father, a grandfather, a king, a religious scholar or a saint).

The excuse of forgetfulness shall not be accepted:

If someone thinks that after being in this world, we no longer remember the said pledge and in case we commit an act of *Shirk* now, we shall not be punished as there is no questioning in forgetfulness. The answer to this notion of theirs is that there are many things a man does not remember but once reminded by a creditable and authentic person, it all comes back to his memory. For instance, no one remembers his date of birth, but once he hears about it from people, he has no qualms about saying it with certainty that I was born on such and such date, in such and such year and at such and such hour. He only recognizes his parents upon hearing from people. He does not consider anyone else as his mother. In case one does not perform his obligations towards his mother and proclaims someone else as his mother, the people are bound to ridicule and censure him. In response to their chidings, if he postulates that as long as I do not remember my birth, why should I consider this woman as my mother? People have no reason to castigate me about it! Once this person blurts out such a statement, people shall definitely regard him to be a perfect moron and a rude person. It thus becomes known to us that since a man believes in many a thing to the extent of certitude on the basis of hearing them merely from

---

the Qur'an with the following statement: (And there was also a time) when We took a pledge from the Prophets. These Prophets include you (Prophet Muhammad {Peace be upon Him} , Noah, Abraham, Moses and Jesus the son of Mary).

people, how is it that he should disbelieve the teachings of the Prophets who are the people of a great status and magnificent caliber!

The basic teachings of the Prophets and the (Divine) Scriptures:

Thus we understand that every one has been individually inculcated and stressed upon in the realms of the spirits to adopt and adhere to the concept of *Tauhid*[1](Monotheism) and shun *Shirk* (polytheism), i.e. associating partners with Allah in the acts belonging to Him. All the Prophets have been sent to this world for the sole purpose of reminding people of this covenant and its renewal. The instructions of more than one hundred and twenty-four thousand Messengers of Allah and the central knowledge contained in all the Divine Scriptures concentrate on just one point, "Beware! the concept of *Tauhid* (Monotheism) should not be tampered with and do not even think of associating partners with Allah! Do not consider anyone as an absolute sovereign and a disposer (of the affairs) except Allah! Do not resort to anyone for the fulfillment of your wishes and making vows except Allah!"

Once we are informed about the following *Hadith,* there is no room left whatsoever for an excuse to commit an act of *Shirk* by anybody. This is how the *Hadith* goes:

It is narrated by Mu'adh bin Jabal {May Allah have mercy on him} that he was instructed by the Prophet {Peace be upon Him} to the effect that:

"You must not join others as partners with Allah even if you are murdered or burnt to death."
(Musnad Ahmad)

This means that we must not consider anyone else other than Allah as worthy of being worshipped and do not care for being molested by a jinn or devil. As the Muslims must patiently bear the brunt of the external calamities, without jeopardizing their Faith, they must also bear the internal inflictions (i.e., molestations on the part of jinns, ghosts and other such beings) with patience without perverting their Faith out of their fright. They should hold the belief that everything whether an affliction or comfort is directly governed by Allah. Allah sometimes puts his faithful believers on trial. A believer is tested according to the strength of his Faith. Sometime pious people are subjected to chastisement on the part of the wicked persons so that a distinction may be established between the sincere and the hypocrite. As the pious are apparently molested by the disobedient ones and the Muslims by the disbelievers (through the Will of Allah) and they continue to bear with it with perseverance and patience without perverting their Faith due to being disgruntled with the trials, similarly the pious are sometimes subjected to trouble on the part of jinns and Satans through the Will of Allah. So one should bear with it steadfastly and patiently without yielding to their hegemony out of the fear of their oppression. Thus it becomes known to us that if a person denies a deity (false deity other than Allah) out of being averse to *Shirk,* repudiates and condemns making vows and offerings to it, removes the erroneous and unjustified customs associated with it; and in the process of doing it, if such a person incurs either a loss of life or a loss in terms of finances, or should Satan happen to chastise him in the name of a preceptor or a martyr (by making such fake appearances), he must understand that Allah is

---

[1] It means declaring Allah to be the only God Who deserves to be worshipped in truth and confirming all attributes with which He has gratified Himself or that are attributed to Him by His Messenger {Peace be upon Him}.

testing his Faith which he must humbly bear with and should hold on to his Faith steadfastly. We must remember that Allah tightens His grip on the oppressors after giving them plenty of rope and liberates the oppressed from their talons, similarly He shall grab on to the oppressors among the jinn in due course of time and shall release the adherents to the concept of Oneness of Allah (the monotheists upholding the cause of *'Tauhid')* from their tyranny.

It has been narrated by Ibn Mas'ud {May Allah have mercy on him}:

"A person enquired of the Prophet {Peace be upon Him} as to which is the biggest of all sins. He said that it is to call upon someone else other than Allah, thinking of him as similar to Allah, even though Allah has created you." (Al-Bukhari-Muslim)

It means that as Allah (on account of His Knowledge and Capability), is believed to be the Omnipresent and the Conductor of the whole universe, and is called upon in times of distress, similarly calling upon some other entity other than Allah believing in it to be characterized by the same qualities is the greatest of all sinful acts. Because none has the capability to solve the problems of creatures except Allah. Furthermore, as long as our *Rabb* is Allah, we must call upon Him Alone in distress situations as we have no link with any other entity. For example, if someone becomes a slave to a king, he is bound to approach his king for the fulfillment of all his needs. Not to speak of a shoe-maker or a sweeper, he will not even approach other kings (for his personal needs). Since there is no entity at all, whatsoever, who could be considered a counterpart of Allah, is it not a folly to approach any other entity for the fulfillment of one's needs?

Tauhid (Monotheism) and forgiveness:

It has been narrated by Anas {May Allah have mercy on him} that the Prophet {Peace be upon Him} said:

"Allah the Exalted states to the posterity of Adam that if you happen to meet Me with the sinful acts of the entire world, I shall meet you with an equal amount of mercy provided you have not joined partners with Me."

It means that there had been many delinquent and sinful people in the world including Pharaoh and Haman etc. as well as Satan, who also is to be found in this world. All these sinners have been committing sins and shall continue committing them till Doomsday. Now, if a person supposedly commits all these sins collectively to his sole account individually, chances are that Allah shall bestow on him an equal amount of mercy and forgiveness, provided he has not committed *Shirk*. Thus it becomes known to us that with the blessing of *Tauhid,* all the sins are forgiven[1] exactly in the same manner as the virtuous deeds are destroyed by the evil of *Shirk*.

---

[1] The purpose of mentioning this *Hadith* here is to clarify that committing an act of *Shirk* is an extremely obnoxious and abominable thing. One should not however, deduce that as long as one is free from *Shirk,* the commission of other sinful acts are in any way justifiable. In regard to the forgiveness of sins, one should take into consideration the general rule of *Shari'ah* (i.e., seeking Allah's forgiveness and becoming repentant).

This is also a fact that when a man is completely cleansed off the impurities of *Shirk* and shall uphold a faith that none but Allah is his Master, and there is no place to flee His Rule, none offers shelter to the ones who disobey Him, all are helpless before Him, none can deter His Commandment, none can intercede with Him on behalf of someone else and no one can make a recommendation before Him for someone without His Permission, -on nursing this set of beliefs - the possibility of sins which might be committed by him could be only either due to his inherent human weaknesses or his forgetfulness. And then such a person shall have been groaning under the burden of these sins, shall be utterly disgusted and shall not be able to raise his head (out of a sense of shame and remorse). This type of person is undoubtedly blessed with the mercy of Allah. As the amount of sins increases, so increases the intensity of his remorse and the more his remorse becomes intense, so does the mercy of Allah.

We must remember the point that the sin of a devout monotheist can do what a virtuous deed of a polytheist cannot. A delinquent monotheist is a thousand times better than an observant and pious polytheist exactly in a similar manner as a criminal subject is a thousand times preferable to a toady mutineer, because the former is remorseful on his sin, and the latter proud and callous.

Chapter Four
The negation of *Shirk* in knowledge

Allah says in one of the Qur'anic verses as follows:

{And with Him are the keys of the *Ghaib* (all that is hidden), none knows them but He. And He knows whatever there is in (or on) the earth and in the sea; not a leaf falls, but He knows it. There is not a grain in the darkness of the earth nor anything fresh or dry, but is written in a Clear Record.} (V.6:59)

It means that Allah has bestowed on the humans some faculties so that they may have an access to the knowledge concerning the apparent on the physical plane; for instance eyes to sight, ears to listen, nose to smell, tongue to taste, hands to grope about, and intellect to understand. Then, the above faculties have been put at the disposal of a human being so that he may utilize them on his own accord; for instance, whenever he intends to see an object, he may open his eyes and whenever he does not intend to see it, he may close them. Other limbs may also be utilized in a similar manner. Human beings have been given the keys to have an access to the knowledge of the evident things. As the matter of doing and undoing a lock mainly depends on the will of its owner, similarly the act of gaining knowledge about the apparent things depends upon the will of a human being.

Only Allah possesses the knowledge of *Ghaib* (unseen and hidden):

Contrary to the above, it is beyond the authority of a human being to gain the knowledge of the unknown, as Allah Himself preserves the keys to it. No entity whatsoever (whether one of the most prominent humans or one of the most eminent angels) has been given an authority to know about the unseen in a manner that they may exercise their own will to gain knowledge about the hidden matters. However, whenever Allah so wishes, He reveals a certain amount of information concerning the Unknown to someone. Giving information about the unknown solely depends on the Will of Allah and not on the desire of someone. On many occasions Allah's Prophet {Peace be upon Him} had a desire to gain knowledge about a certain thing or occurrence, which he could not know, but the same was revealed to him whenever Allah intended to do so. During the era of Prophethood, the hypocrites slandered `Aisha {May Allah have mercy on Her} which shocked the Prophet {Peace be upon Him} tremendously. He tried- to probe into the matter for -many days, but failed to ferret out the truth. And when Allah intended, the Prophet was informed through the process of revelation that the hypocrites are none but liars and the chastity of 'Aisha Siddiqah {May Allah have mercy on her} was verily beyond reproach. A Muslim monotheist must have a conviction that Allah preserves the keys to the treasures of the unknown with none but Himself and has appointed none as their treasurer. No one can stop Him if He Himself awards something to whomsoever He so wishes (by Himself unlocking one of His treasures).

The one who claims to have the knowledge of *Ghaib* (unseen), is a liar:

We thus understand that anyone who claims to possess a certain art or knowledge enabling him to have a peep into the *Ghaib*, to reveal the past incidents and to adumbrate about the futuristic events, is an outright liar claiming godship. In case someone recognizes a Prophet, a saint, a jinn, an angel, an *Imam*, a man of piety, a religious preceptor, a martyr, an astrologer, a seer, a clairvoyant, a prestidigitator, a pundit, a ghost, or a fairy to be as such (having the knowledge of the unknown), such a person becomes a *Mushrik*, and he (rejects and negates) denies the contents of the above verses. Even if a certain prediction of an astronomer, by a sheer chance, happens to come true, it does not prove his knowledge of the unknown because most of their statements turn out to be incorrect. Hence we understand that it is beyond their capacity to have a knowledge of the *Ghaib*. A conjectural utterance may at times prove to be correct and at times incorrect. The same is also true in regard to making Prophecies, getting the things known through a Divine Inspiration, or resorting the Qur'anic verses to gain an insight into the future events. A revelation, however, is never incorrect and is not under their control. Allah reveals whatever He intends to, out of His Own Free Will. A revelation does not depend on the desire of anyone. Allah the Exalted says:

{Say: 'None in the heavens and the earth knows the *Ghaib* (unseen) except Allah, nor can they perceive when they shall be resurrected.}(V.27:65)

It means that no one has the capability to have an access to the knowledge of the *Ghaib* whether he is one of the most prestigious human beings or one of the most high-ranking angels. This fact may be corroborated by the evidence that the whole world knows about the advent of the Doomsday, but none of them knows as to when shall it occur! Had they been possessing the capability to gain knowledge of everything, they would have known the date of its advent also!

The matters of *Ghaib* (the unknown and unseen):

Allah the Almighty says:

{Verily, Allah! With Him (alone) is the knowledge of the Hour, He sends down the rain, and knows that which is in the wombs. No person knows what he will earn tomorrow, and no person knows in what land he will die. Verily, Allah is All-Knower, All-Aware (of things.} (V.31:34)

It means that Allah Alone knows the matters of the *Ghaib*. While no one other than Him has the knowledge of the unseen. Nobody knows as to when shall the Doomsday occur, a news so much wide-spread and well-known among the people that they are almost certain about its occurrence, what about the matters like victory and defeat, health and sickness and (others like it) similar to it. No one knows about them either. These matters are neither well-known like the Doomsday nor are absolutely definite. Similarly, nobody knows when shall it start raining even though it has a definite season and it often rains during that season. Most of people do wish to know about it and had it been possible to know it beforehand, they would indeed have known about it. Then how could the people possibly know about the things which neither belong to a particular season nor are they of any public interest like someone's death and his life-span, being blessed with a child or not, being wealthy or impoverished, emerging victorious or facing an ignominy of defeat etc. No one knows as to whether a womb carries one or more than one child[1], whether a fetus is a male one or a female one, complete or defective, beautiful or ugly, even though the physicians do

---

[1] Even the contemporary medical science can determine the sex of the fetus only in case it happens to be in the last stages of its birth.

narrate the reasons causing different formations and configurations, but they do not know about someone's particular case. In such a case, how could one possibly read the internal matters of a person like thoughts, intentions and the condition of one's Faith and hypocrisy. As long as one does not know as to what he himself shall be doing tomorrow, how could he know about the circumstances of others and since a man does not even have an inkling about the place of his death, how could he have a fore-knowledge about the day and time of his passing away. Be it as it may, no person or entity has the capability to learn about the future by exercising his own free will and choice except Allah. Hence it becomes known to us that the people who claim to have the knowledge of the unseen are none but liars. The so-called concepts and methods of learning about what is unseen like a Divine inspiration, soothsaying, foretelling by figures, astronomy, divination and casting lots are none but falsehood and are only Satanic tricks and illusions. Muslims should not be entangled with them and give them no credit at all. And if someone neither claims to possess the knowledge of the unseen nor claims to have the capability of knowing it by exercising his own free will but he only claims that a certain matter which Allah has informed him about, was beyond his control and capacity; and his own choice and will, had nothing to do with it; in this case there are both the possibilities, the man making such a statement, could either be truthful or a liar.

Do not call upon anyone but Allah: Allah says:

{And who is more stray than one who calls (invokes) besides Allah, such as will not answer him till the Day of Resurrection, and who are (even) unaware of their calls (invocations) to them?}
(V.46:5)

It means that the polytheists are an extremely idiotic bunch of people, who, by avoiding Allah (who possesses all authority and knowledge) invoke the other so-called deities who neither hear their invocations nor are capable of doing anything. Even if they keep calling them till the Doomsday, those (so-called) deities would not respond to their calls. Thus we may deduce that the people who call upon the men of piety from a certain distance by only requesting them to pray to Allah for them so that Allah may fulfill their wishes, also commit an act of *Shirk* even though they may not think it to be as such, since the prayer of fulfillment is eventually directed to Allah. But in fact, this act has become tainted with *Shirk* as a third person has been called upon with the belief that this person possesses the capability of hearing from far and near (if invoked), whereas it is a quality which is attributed to Allah Alone. Allah Himself says that they (deities etc.) are unaware of their calls (invocations) to them. They do not hear the invocations of a caller even if he keeps shouting (his invocations) until the Doomsday.

Allah Alone, possesses the power of benefit and inflicting harm:

{Say (O Muhammad {Peace be upon Him}): "I possess no power of benefit or hurt to myself except as Allah wills. If I had the knowledge of the *Ghaib* (unseen), I should have secured for myself an abundance of wealth, and no evil should have touched me. I am but a warner, and a bringer of glad tidings unto people who believe."}(V. 7: 188)

The Prophet {Peace be upon Him}is the leader of all the Prophets. Many miracles are ascribed to him and people learned the subtleties and nuances of religion from him. People acquired piety and virtuosity by following his prescribed path. Allah Himself I instructed him to give people an account of his helplessness making it clearly known to the people that he is neither capable of exercising any authority nor possesses any knowledge of the unseen. One can easily run a conjecture from the fact that as long as he does not even possess an authority to gain a certain advantage for himself or to ward off an evil from inflicting him, how could he benefit or harm someone else. Had he been having the knowledge of the unseen, he would have known about the results of a certain action beforehand even prior to undertaking it, and if he had a faintest premonition that the result of a certain action is going to be unfavorable, he would not have undertaken that action at all. The knowledge of the unseen is one of the Attributes of Allah and he is merely a Messenger. The mission of a Messenger is only confined to warning people about the dire consequences of bad actions and to give people glad tidings about virtuous deeds. This too benefits the ones who nurse such a Belief *(Tauhid)* in their hearts and the nurturing of such a Belief is also one of the Qualities of Allah.

The original assignment of the Prophets:

It becomes known to us that the greatness of the Prophets and saints epitomizes in the fact that they direct people to the path of Allah and give people information about whatever good and bad deeds they are themselves informed of. Allah has endowed their propagation with a quality of a convincing effectiveness. Many people are directed to the Right Path through their efforts. No such authority has been conferred on them that they should personally conduct and dispose off the worldly matters like causing death to someone, bless someone with a son or daughter, warding off an evil, fulfillment of one's wishes, crowning someone with success or destine someone to defeat, granting someone riches or making someone indigent and impoverished, turning someone into either a king or a mendicant, transforming someone into a nobleman and minister or turning someone into a poor and dejected person, kindling the spark of Faith in someone's heart or having the same snatched away from him, or turning a healthy person into a sick person and sick person into a healthy one. These attributes belong to Allah only and everybody, regardless of his status, is unable to do such things except Allah. Everyone is treated on an equal footing in terms of this inability.

The Prophets do not have the knowledge of the unseen:

The Prophets do not enjoy the distinction of having been awarded the keys to the unseen to the effect that they may have a cognizance of someone's innermost feelings or could make predictions about whether or not someone is going to be blessed with a child, whether one's business is going to yield profit or incur a loss, or whether someone is going to emerge victorious in a battlefield or face a defeat. As far as the above things are concerned, everybody is equally unaware about them regardless of his status. However, certain remarks which are made in reference to a certain context out of one's wisdom do sometimes come true. Similarly, these eminent people (i.e., the Prophets) make certain remarks in relation to a certain context using their own wisdom which sometimes prove to be correct and sometimes incorrect. But whatever information a Prophet is given through Divine Revelation is never incorrect, but the Revelation does not depend on a Prophet's own will.

The sayings of the Prophet {Peace be upon Him} regarding the knowledge of the unseen:

It has been narrated by Rubai' bint Muawwidh bin' Afra[1]:

---

[1] 'Afra is the name of the mother of `Auf, Muawwidh and Mu'adh {May Allah have mercy on him}.'Afra {May Allah have mercy on him} had six sons, all of whom participated in the battle of Badr. Two of them were killed as martyrs in the battle of Badr. Mu'adh and Muawwidh {May Allah have mercy on him} jointly killed Abu Jahl.

"The Prophet {Peace be upon Him} came to me while I was about to depart to my husband's house (after the completion of marriage ceremony) and sat next to me on my bed. Some of our young girls, to the accompaniment of the sound of a drumbeat, started narrating the saga of our martyrs during the battle of Badr. One of them even went to the extent of saying that our Prophet (who is amongst us) knows what is going to happen tomorrow. He (the Prophet {Peace be upon Him} said, "Stop what you are saying now and say what you have been saying before." (Al-Bukhari)

It means that on the occasion of Rubayi `Ansariya' s marriage ceremony, Prophet {Peace be upon Him} sat by her side. While singing frolickingly, the young girls made a remark saying that our Prophet knows what is going to happen tomorrow. The Prophet {Peace be upon Him} prohibited them from making such an utterance and asked them to refrain from it thenceforth. It thus becomes clearly known that a person no matter how pious and virtuous he is, we must not believe that he has the knowledge of the unseen. The poets, who keep eulogizing the Prophet {Peace be upon Him} by writing panegyric and laudatory poems extolling him to the skies and thereby justifying their uncalled for eloquence under the pretext of a mere exaggeration, is absolutely inc9rrect. So long as the Prophet {Peace be upon Him} did not even allow the young girls to recite verses in his praise, how could it be justifiable for an intellectual poet to verbalize or listen to such verses.

The saying of Aisha {May Allah have mercy on Her}:

Aisha {May Allah have mercy on Her} stated:

"Whosoever ascribes the knowledge of five things to Allah's Prophet Muhammad {Peace be upon Him} which Allah has referred to in the verse saying: Allah has the knowledge of the Hour," (V.31:34), has attributed to him a monstrous calumny." (Al-Bukhari)

It means that all the matters related to the unseen are covered under these five things that are stated at the end of *Surah* Luqman and mentioned earlier. Therefore, whoever says that the Prophet {Peace be upon Him} knew all the things belonging to the realms of the unknown, has indeed committed an immensely slanderous act. None has the knowledge of the *Ghaib* except Allah.

It has been reported by Umm Ala {May Allah have mercy on her} that the Prophet {Peace be upon Him} said:

"Even though I am a Messenger of Allah, I can say swearingly by Him in the earnest, that I do not have a faintest idea as to what is going to happen to me or to you." (Al-Bukhari)

It implies that the kind of treatment Allah is going to mete out to his slaves in this world, in their graves, or in the Hereafter is neither known by a Prophet, nor a sage. They neither know about themselves nor about the others. If someone happens to know about a certain person through Revelation that he is going to have a happy ending, such a piece of information thus acquired (through Revelation) is regarded to be no more than a brief and superficial knowledge. Acquiring any further knowledge is beyond their capacity.

Chapter Five
The Negation of *Shirk* in Authority

Allah says:

{Say: In Whose Hand is the sovereignty of everything (i.e. treasures of each and everything)? And He protects (all), while against Whom there is no protector, (i.e. if Allah saves anyone none can punish or harm him, and if Allah punishes or harms anyone none can save him), if you know. They will say: '(All that belongs) to Allah.' Say: How then are you deceived and turn away from the truth?}(V.23:88, 89)

It means that even if a *Mushrik* (polytheist) is questioned as to who is the one who has an absolute authority and command to conduct and dispose off the worldly affairs in whatever way he pleases and there is none who could deter or circumvent Him, they will say that it is verily Allah the Almighty. As long as this is the ultimate truth, isn't it a lunacy to entreat other entities (other than Allah) and request them for the fulfillment of ones desires! We must also bear in mind that even during the era of the Prophet {Peace be upon Him}, there were people who believed that there is no counterpart of Allah and there is none who could equal Him but they still worshipped idols considering them as their intercessors and asked them for the fulfillment of their wishes, and hence became *Mushrik* (polytheists). Even today, if someone believes that any other entity (other than Allah) exercises it's authority in disposing off the worldly affairs and worships it as his intercessor, he will become a *Mushrik* even though he does not regard it to be as Allah's equal in the matter of withstanding His Might.

Allah is the One Who causes benefit and inflicts harm:

Allah the Almighty says:

{Say: 'It is not my power to cause you harm, or bring you to the Right Path.' Say (O Muhammad {Peace be upon Him}: "None can protect me from Allah's punishment (if I were to disobey Him), nor should I find refuge except in Him."}(V.72:21, 22)

It means that the matters which are either beneficial to you or are detrimental to your interests are beyond my (the Prophet's) control. You must not exceed the limits and become proud by harboring a fallacy that as you are my followers, you have a strong base and you enjoy the privilege of having a strong advocate and a beloved intercessor, you are free to do according to the dictates of your whims and I will eventually save you from the perdition of Allah. But the case is that I myself happen to be at His mercy and see no refuge except with Him Alone, how could I save others from punishment. It thus becomes clear that the ones who forget Allah by banking on the religious preceptors and thereby defying His Instructions, have indeed strayed from the Right Path, because the Prophet {Peace be upon Him} used to fear Allah day and night and could see his refuge with none but Allah. Since the Prophet {Peace be upon Him} was himself meticulously observant about these matters, how could any so and-so may even think of the possibility of being exonerated from punishment despite committing sinful acts.

None is the sustainer except Allah:

Allah the Exalted says:

{And they worship others besides Allah, -such as do not and cannot own any provision for them from the heavens or the earth.}(V.16:73)

It means that the people accord them such a respect and honor as deserved by Allah only, even though they have nothing to do with providing them any livelihood. Neither can they induce rain nor can they grow anything from the earth. They are devoid of any capability whatsoever. It is amazing to notice a popular fallacy among the masses that the sages, even though possessing a capability of exercising authority in the day-to-day worldly matters, they do not interfere in these matters out of a sense of respectfulness, and are contented with the Divine destiny. Otherwise, they can make the whole universe upside down if they so wish, but thinking of the enormity of evil and a havoc which could be wrought by such an action, they keep mum and maintain their composure. This idea is absolutely incorrect. They are not capable of doing that either in terms of action or power. In other words, they do not possess any capability and power to exercise such kind of authority.

Invoke none but Allah:

Allah the Almighty says:

{And invoke not besides Allah, any that will neither profit you, nor hurt you, but if (in case) you did so, you shall certainly be one of the *Zalimun* (polytheists and wrong doers)} (V.10:106)

It means that in the presence of Allah, who is the Lord of all the majesty, honor and magnificence, calling upon such incapacitated entities who can neither profit nor hurt anyone is truly a wrongful act for the simple reason that a position of honor, which is the prerogative of the greatest only, is being given to the riffraff among the people who are not worth their salt.

Allah says:

{Say: (O Muhammad {Peace be upon Him} to those polytheists, pagans, etc.) "Call upon those whom you assert (to be associate gods) besides Allah, they possess not even the weight of an atom (or a small ant), -either in the heavens or on the earth, nor have they any share in either, nor there is for Him any supporter from among them.' Intercession with Him profits not, except for him whom He permits.[1] Until when fear is banished from their (angels') hearts, they (angels) say:

---

[1] It implies that the intercessor as well the intercessed had been frantically waiting for the approval. Once the approval was granted, they had been asking each other as to what their Lord had said. This is a psychological situation which will overwhelm everybody where they will be asking each other in an amazed stupefaction as to whether or not the permission of their Lord has been granted?

'What is that your Lord has said?' They say: 'The truth.' And He is the Most High, the Most Great.}(V.34:22,23)

No intercession without His Permission:

There are several forms involved in asking someone for the fulfillment of one's desires in distress situations and getting the same fulfilled by him. It could be that the person so requested is himself the master, or a partner of the master, or has influence upon the master himself, as a king may concede to the opinions of his deputies (in their capacity of being the pillars of the empire) as making them displeased jeopardizes the administration of the government, or a situation wherein a person happens to intercede with his master for someone which the master dares not refuse and willy-nilly becomes obliged to accord his approval, like the princesses or the queens whose love is cherished by a king and as such can not reject an intercession made by them out of their love.

Now, let us think about the polytheists who despite Allah, call upon the saints and ask them to fulfill their wishes. These saints do not even own a pittance in the universe nor they have a wee bit of share in it. They are neither the pillars of the Divine empire nor are they assistants and helpers to Allah the Almighty so that Allah succumbs to their pressurization and concedes to whatever they say. They can not even utter a word in regard to someone's intercession without the permission of Allah Himself and may acquire nothing for anyone. Once they happen to be in the presence of Allah and hear His Commandment, they become so much awe-inspired and instilled with fear that they almost lose their senses. They do not even dare speak to Allah to reconfirm His Statement out of respect and being overpowered by fright, but they ask each other as to what their Lord has said, and once they confirm it, they will have to believe it and testify to it and hence the question of daring to make an intercession or playing an advocate on someone else's behalf does not arise.

Types of intercession:

The most important thing which we must bear in mind is that the masses take pride in the intercession (which they believe shall) to be made by the Prophets and saints for them on the Day of Judgment. They have forgotten Allah by having misunderstood the meaning of *Shafa'ah*. In fact *Shafa'ah* means 'interceding with someone on someone else's behalf'. In this world, there are many forms of making an intercession. For example, a felony of theft committed by a thief becomes proven in the sight of a king and a deputy or a minister mediates with the king and saves him from punishment which he has incurred due to crime. In this situation, the king did intend to punish the miscreant in accordance with the law of the country, but as long as the king honors the minister's word, he acquits the thief and lets him go unpunished. The king does so because the minister is one of the pillars on which his whole kingdom is based upon and he does not want make the minister displeased lest his displeasure should jeopardize the organizational machinery of the government. Taking all these matters into his consideration, the king thus suppresses his anger and forgives the thief. This type of intercession is known as *Shafa'at-e-Wajahat* which means that the request of the minister has been granted due to his honor and high-ranking status.

An intercession due to one's high-ranking status is not possible:

An intercession by someone, enjoying a high-ranking status and the one who is dear and near to Allah, is utterly impossible. A person who recognizes an entity (other than Allah) to be such kind of mediator, is definitely a polytheist and undoubtedly an ignorant person. He has not understood the meaning of *Ilah* (God) and has not appreciated the status of the King of kings at all. Allah's Status is so Great and Exalted that if He so wishes, He may bring into existence millions of Prophets, saints, jinns, angels, and entities equal to Gabriel and Prophet Muhammad {Peace be upon Him} in terms of status, merely by uttering a word "Be," He can decimate all the universe including heavens and earth within a blinking of an eye and create a different world. Everything comes into existence merely by His Will and He does not require matter and substance to create things. If all the human beings and jinns right from the era of Adam {Peace be upon Him} and until the Doomsday, altogether become like Gabriel and Prophets (in terms of piety and virtuosity), it will not add up an iota in the grandeur of Allah's empire and if all of them turn into devils and antichrists (in terms of disobedience and vices), there shall still be no reduction in the magnificence of His empire. In any case, He will still continue to be the Greatest of all and the King of all kings. No one can either harm Him or benefit Him.

There is also a *Hadith* to this end which says:

"O my slaves! In case all among you (the jinns and humans) who have passed away and the ones who shall be born in future in unison become like the one who is the most pious among you all, you must remember that it will add up nothing in my empire. Similarly, if you collectively (including the ones who have passed away as well as the oncoming generations) become vice-ridden and sinners like the one worst among you all, it shall effect no reduction at all in my kingdom."

Acceptance of one's intercession out of love is not possible:

Another type of interceding is that a prince, a queen or a beloved of the king comes forward and does not let the king punish a thief. The king, out of his love for the person in question, does not wish to make him displeased and therefore, grants a pardon to the thief. This kind of intercession is known as an acceptance of intercession granted out of love for the person concerned. The king, being driven by the love of the concerned person, takes into account the fact that invoking a beloved's displeasure shall in turn inflict pain on himself and hence he concedes to the request of his beloved. This kind of occurrence in the court of Allah the Almighty is impossible. If someone reckons a prophet or a saint to be this kind of intercessor, he also is a pure polytheist and an utterly ignorant person. Allah, the King of kings, may reward his slaves by honoring them in whatever manner He pleases, may confer grand titles on them like *Habib* (the beloved), *Khalil* (the friend), *Kalim* (conversant), *Ruhullah* (Allah's spirit) and *Wajih* (the good-looking). Likewise He may bestow on His slaves such titles of honor as *Rasul Karim* (a kind messenger), *Makin* (the high rank). *Ruhul-Quds* (the holy spirit) and *Ruhul-Amin* (the honest spirit). But it should be in mind that a master is after all, a master and a slave is after all a slave. (They are poles apart). Each one has a specified limit. As a slave becomes enraptured in pondering over the bliss of His mercy, he also becomes overwhelmed with a feeling of fright when he happens to think about His overpowering greatness.

Interceding with permission:

The third kind of intercession implies the situation wherein a thief indeed is found guilty of theft but he has not committed it by way of profession but he has unfortunately slipped into it (being a victim of circumstances). Out of a feeling of guilt, this person now feels extremely remorseful, his head lowered downward, constantly being gnawed by the fear of punishment. Paying due respect to the law of the land, he considers himself to be vice-ridden, a perpetrator of sin and thus eligible for punishment.

He does not flee the king and does not request a courtier or a minister to intercede with the king for his amnesty. He seeks no one's support other than the king himself. He only pins his hopes to His Majesty day in and day out and is awaiting the pronouncement of a judgment in regard to the delinquency. The king, taking pity on his deplorable condition, intends to connive at his delinquency but also wants to uphold the law of the country lest it should be looked down upon by the people. Now, a governor or a minister, after getting a wink from the king, comes forward to intercede on his behalf. So the king grants a pardon to the thief apparently on the plea that so long as the governor has himself interceded for him, he has to honor it. The governor did not intercede for the thief because he was either his relative, friend or one of his acquaintances or he took the responsibility of defending him, but it was simply due to the fact that the king willingly instructed him to do so. Obviously, he is a governor appointed by the king and not a supporter of the thief (and hence he will not undertake an action of this kind without a nod of approval from the king), as the one who favors a thief is himself a thief. This type of intercession is known as "an intercession with permission" (mediation with the permission and willingness of the master himself). This kind of intercession only shall prevail in the court of Allah the Almighty. An intercession by a Prophet or a saint which is mentioned in the Noble Qur'an is none other than this type of intercession.

The Straight Path:

It is obligatory on every human being to call upon none but Allah Alone, must fear Him all the time and keep seeking His forgiveness from sins regularly. One must confess to having committed sins before Him Alone and consider Him Alone to be one's master and supporter. One should seek refuge in none but Allah and must not depend on anyone's support, as our Lord is All-Forgiver and Most Compassionate. Out of His sheer blessing and mercy, He will obviate all our miseries and forgive all our sins. Whomsoever He wishes, shall appoint as your intercessor on His own instruction. As you entrust Him with the fulfillment of all your needs, so should you entrust Him with the responsibility of assigning anyone as your intercessor whosoever He wishes. Never depend on anyone's support. Call upon Him Alone to lend you support. Never forget the real Master. Appreciate and pay due deference to the rulings of *Shari 'ah* (Islamic law) and disregard the established social customs and traditions (in case they happen to be in a direct confrontation with the rulings of *Shari'ah*). Abiding by the social mores by disregarding the injunctions of *Shari 'ah* is an extremely severe crime.

All the Prophets and saints are averse to it. They never intercede on behalf of someone who adhere to the social customs and defy the injunctions of *Shari'ah*. On the contrary, they become opposed to such people and become displeased with them, because their piety only rested on the factor that they accorded every preference to the willingness of Allah. They used to abandon their wives, children, followers, disciples, servants and friends for the sake of Allah and whenever those people used to do anything contrary to the Will of Allah, they turned into their enemies. What goodness of polytheists could attract the people of eminence to be their intercessors with Allah and engage themselves in a heated discussion with Him for their sake? Such a thing is never bound to happen as they (i.e. Prophets and saints) are their enemies. Loving and contradicting people for the sake of Allah only, is the quality they are characterized with. In case Allah does intend to make someone taste the Hell-fire, they shall be only prepared to fell him into the Hell-fire by dealing him a few blows and pushes. They are merely dependent on the Will of Allah and shall irresistibly tilt towards it.

It is reported by Ibn Abbas {May Allah have mercy on him}:

"One day I was behind the Prophet {Peace be upon Him}.He addressed me and said, 'O boy! Remember Allah and Allah shall remember you. Remember Allah and you shall see Him right before you. Whenever you ask for anything, ask it from Allah and whenever you look for assistance, do it by requesting Allah Alone. Be certain that if all the people collectively agree to do you a benefit, they shall not be able to do more than what Allah has preordained for you and in case they all agree to inflict harm on you, they would not do it more than what Allah has in store for you. The pens have been lifted and the books have gone dry." (Tirmidhi)

It means that Allah the Almighty is truly and justifiably the King of all kings. He is not proud (and haughty) like the kings of the world as they do not pay any heed to the pleadings of any of their subjects due to an empty sense of conceit. It is only due to this reason that if the general people were to ask for anything from the king, they do it through his deputies instead of having a direct audience with the king himself so that their request be granted for their sake, at least.

But Allah is far above this type of categorization. On the contrary, He is Extremely Beneficent and Most Merciful. In order to attract His attention, no one's mediation is required. He takes care of everyone individually and remembers everyone regardless whether or not someone intercedes for him. He is Pure, Supreme and Far Exalted from the rest. His Court is unlike the courts of the worldly kings wherein the people in general are unable to have an access to the royal court; only the king's deputies themselves exercise their authority on the public and the subjects having no option but to obey their orders. On the contrary, it is the Divine court and Allah is far nearer to His slaves. An ordinary man, who turns to Him and focuses his attention onto Him by the depths of his heart, would find Him near himself. There is no veil between a slave and Allah except (the curtain of) his own negligence.[1]

Allah is the Nearest to all:

If someone happens to be away from Allah, it is only due to his own negligence. Otherwise the *Rabb* is very nearer to all.

Anyone calling upon a Prophet or a saint with the notion that they shall draw him near Allah, do not understand the fact that a distance however, is wedged between him and a saint or a Prophet, whereas Allah is in fact very very close to him. We can understand it through this example:

Let us suppose that a slave stands alone in the presence of the king who is all ears to listen to him,

---

[1] *'Al-Qadar* (Destiny) is another name for the Divine knowledge. No human being can know as to what is written in his own or someone's else's destiny. Therefore, it is the first and last obligation on every human being to strictly observe the Divine injunctions and interdictions (following Allah's Instructions and avoiding things which He forbade), and should look forward to all goodness out of His mercy.

but he instead, calls one of the deputies loudly and request him to convey his request to the attention of His Majesty. What do you think of this slave now? Obviously he is either blind or crazy! Everyone must ask Allah Alone and must seek His Help Alone in distress. One must be absolutely certain that whatever has already been written down in one's destiny may not be erased. In case the world to its entirety becomes incumbent on benefiting or harming someone, they can do it no more than what has already been written in his destiny. Thus it becomes abundantly clear that no one has the capability of effecting a change in one's fate. A person who has no children in his destiny, who can bless him with children and the one who has already completed his life-span, who can grant him a lease of life? Therefore, whoever maintains that Allah has empowered His saints to effect a change in someone's destiny is quite incorrect. The fact is that Allah grants His approvals to the invocations of everyone among His slaves sometimes only, whereas He certainly accords His approval to most of the supplications made by the Prophets and saints. He is the One who guides someone to offer supplications to Him and He Himself approves of them. Making a supplication and getting the same approved are both preordained and inscribed in one's fate. Nothing in the world happens outside the sphere and realms of fate and no one, regardless of his big and small status, or whether he is a Prophet or a saint, is capable of doing anything. All one can do is praying to Allah. Now He has the option of either according His approval to it or denying it as a matter of wisdom and precaution.

Trust in Allah Alone:
It has been reported by Ibn Majah on the authority of Amr bin Al-Aas {peace be upon him} that the Prophet {Peace be upon Him} said:

> "Every human heart has a way (i.e. an option) in every field. The one who lets his heart pursue all the avenues, Allah shall not pay any heed to such a person as to in which avenue he has been destroyed. The one who has a complete trust in Allah, He will suffice him in all the avenues."
> (Ibn Majah).

It means that whenever a person is entangled in a distress, or stands in need of something, his thoughts wander around in all directions. His mind entertain different ideas, like invoking a certain Prophet, an *Imam,* a preceptor, a martyr or a fairy. He thinks about consulting an astronomer, a seer, a soothsayer or asking a priest to suggest a way of success for him by casting lots etc. Then the one who runs after every thought, Allah becomes impervious to his supplications and does not include him in the list of his sincere and faithful slaves and thus he loses any chance of being directed and led to the Right Path by Allah. Eventually such a person gets destroyed as a result of running after these thoughts. Someone turns into an atheist, someone becomes an apostate whereas someone else negates and rejects everything believing in nothing at all. However, the one who trusts in Allah and does not run after any fancy is truly a beloved slave of Allah. The avenues of His directions are open to him and his heart becomes blessed with such a quiet, calmness and bliss as can never be achieved by the ones running after their (fleeting) fancies. Whatever is written in one's destiny is bound to happen but the ones who run after thoughts are constantly plagued with trouble whereas the ones having trust in Allah rest in peace.[1]

---

[1] It is reported on the authority of Anas {May Allah have mercy on him} that the Prophet{Peace be upon Him} said:

Do not consider Allah on an equal footing with the worldly kings who do all the major functions by themselves and let their servants perform the menial jobs and hence the people are bound to entreat these servants for the mere trifles. But the management of Allah is a far cry from it. Allah is Omnipotent and within a twinkling of an eye, can ameliorate, treat and rectify innumerable matters. None is a partner in His dominion and sovereignty, none shares His authority; and therefore, no matter how minute and negligible a thing could be, one should demand it directly from Him. No one other than Him can give anything to anyone either big or small.

Relationship does not benefit:
It is reported by Abu Hurairah {May Allah have mercy on him} that when the verse "And warn your tribe of near kindred" (V.26:214) was revealed, the called his relatives and addressed them in the following manner:

"O the progeny of Ka'b bin Luwai! Save your selves from (the torment of) the Hell-fire, for I will not help you in rescuing you from the torment of Allah! 0 the progeny of Murrah bin Ka'b! Save your selves from (the torment of) the Hell-fire, for I will not avail you in (the matter of) rescuing you from the torment of Allah! O the progeny of 'Abd Shams! Save your selves from (the torment of) the Hell-fire, for I will not avail you in (the matter of) rescuing you from the torment of Allah! O the progeny of 'Abd Manafl Save your selves from (the torment of) the Hell-fire, for I will not avail you in (the matter of) rescuing you from the torment of Allah! O the progeny of Hashim! Save your selves from (the torment of) the Hellfire, for I will not avail you in (the matter of) rescuing you from the torment of Allah! 0 the progeny of Abdul Muttalib! Save your selves from (the torment of) the Hellfire, for I will not avail you in (the matter of) rescuing you from the torment of Allah! O Fatimah! Save your self from the (the torment of) Hell-fire! Take whatever you like to take of my property, because I shall not be able to rescue you from the torment of Allah at all!" (Al-Bukhari -Muslim)

It means that the ones who happen to be the relatives of a saint, they become confident of their support and therefore become proud and fearless. Therefore, Allah has enjoined upon His beloved Prophet {Peace be upon Him} to warn his relatives regarding this matter accordingly. He (the Prophet {Peace be upon Him} made it conspicuously clear to all, even to his beloved daughter that a relation only may help in matters which lie under one's control and possession. As regards my belongings, those are at my disposal, I can dispense with them without being miserly but as regards the matters concerning Allah, they are far beyond my power and authority, I can neither vouch for anyone nor could I mediate for him. Everyone must gird up his loins to face the Day of Judgment and must think of rescuing himself from the Hell-fire. It thus becomes known to us that being a relative of a pious man and a saint, does not exonerate anyone from the accountability of his deeds towards Allah. As long as a man does not take it upon himself to perform good deeds, it is difficult for him to pull through

---

"Every Muslim must ask for the fulfillment of his entire needs from his *Rabb,* to the extent that even if he is in need of salt, he should ask his *Rabb* for it and if one of his shoe-laces breaks off, he must still ask his *Rabb* for it." (Tirmidhi)

Chapter Six
Prohibition of *Shirk* in Worship

The definition of worship:

'Ibadah (worship) implies those activities which Allah the Almighty has specified and taught to His slaves for His honor and gratification. Here, we are going to explain as to what those activities are, which Allah has ordained us to perform in His honor so that we should not perform them for any entity other than Allah and thus avoid committing the *Shirk*.

Worship is meant for Allah Alone:

"And indeed We sent Noah to his people (and he said): 'I have come to you as a plain warner. That you worship none but Allah, surely I fear for you the torment of a painful Day.'" (V.11:25, 26)

It means that there has always been a strife between believers and the non-believers ever since the Prophet Noah {Peace be upon Him} was sent to this earth. The beloved slaves of Allah have always maintained and spread the word that we should never express our reverence to any entity, whatsoever, in a manner which is strictly prescribed for Allah, and the acts which have been outlined and delineated to show our respect to Allah only, must not be performed to propitiate any other entity.

Prostration is for Allah only:

Allah says:

{Prostrate not to the sun nor to the moon, but prostrate to Allah who created them, if you (really) worship Him.} (V.41:37)

This verse explains that in Islam, the prostration is the right of the Creator only and therefore, we should not prostrate to any creature, be it the moon, the sun, a Prophet, a saint, a jinn or any angel. If someone maintains that making a prostration to a creature was permissible in the earlier religions, for instance, the angels prostrated to Adam {Peace be upon Him} and Prophet Jacob {Peace be upon Him} prostrated to Prophet Joseph {Peace be upon Him} and hence there is no harm if we make a prostration to a saint as a token of showing our respect to him. We must remember that such a thing proves and confirms one's *Shirk* and thoroughly deprives him of Faith. According to the laws which were prevalent during the period of Adam {Peace be upon Him}, it was permissible to marry one's sisters. Presenting this fact as an evidence, what is the harm if these people marry their sisters. But harm does certainly lie there, because the incestuous relationship with one's sisters is a matter which is forbidden forever and is not permissible under any circumstances. The crux of the matter is that a human being must comply with the instructions of Allah. Any Divine injunction should be acknowledged and acted upon without reluctance and without engaging oneself in a controversial argumentation by employing phony excuses like saying: "It was not ordained to the earlier people, why the same has been forced down our necks?" This type of argumentation leads one into being a disbeliever. To elaborate it further, let us presume that a certain statute was put into effect by a king which was being observed for a long time. Now the legislators replaced it with another law by abrogating the former one, and therefore, it is now necessary to enact this new law and to abide by it. If someone insists that he will only recognize the old law and not the new one, such a person shall be deemed a rebel and a rebel is punishable with imprisonment. Similarly, Hell-fire is the punishment for the ones who rebel against Allah's authority.

It is an act of *Shirk* to call upon anyone other than Allah:

Allah the Almighty says:

> {And the mosques are for Allah (Alone), so invoke not anyone along with Allah! (It has been revealed to me that) When the slave of Allah (Muhammad {Peace be upon Him}) stood up invoking (his Lord-Allah) in prayer to Him they (the jinns) just made round him a dense crown as if sticking one over the other (in order to listen to Prophet's recitation. Say (O Muhammad {Peace be upon Him}): 'I invoke only my Lord (Allah Alone), and I associate none as partners along with Him.'}(V. 72: 18-20)

It means that whenever a slave invokes Allah with a clean and pure heart, these ignorants think that this person is one of the most eminent saints who has been raised to such an exalted status (of being a *Ghauth* or *Qutub)* that he is empowered to grant almost anything to anyone and similarly may deprive anyone of anything whatever he likes. Hence these people form dense crowds around him with the hope that this man would solve their problems and make them overcome their distress. Now, it is an obligation on this man to inform the people about the right thing that one should invoke only Allah during difficult times. This right (the right of being called upon) only belongs to Allah. Any anticipation regarding a profit or loss must be associated with the Will of Allah because attributing such a thing to anyone other than Allah is an act of *Shirk*. I am disgusted with the *Shirk* and its committers. And if someone wants to give me this kind of treatment, I become displeased with him. The acts of granting and taking away belong to Allah the Almighty. This pious person should make it clear to the people that he has no power and authority to do anything. Allah indeed is my *Rabb* and yours, and therefore, we must renounce the false objects of worship and invoke the Lord Who is the Solitary and Unique One having no associates with Him. He is alone in His Oneness, His right of being worshipped, His Lordship and absolute ruling. Thus it becomes known to us that standing with respect (with hands knotted to each other), making an invocation and reciting a certain formula (with repetitions) are the activities which Allah has exclusively specified to be performed in His honor only. According such a treatment to anyone other than Allah is an act of *Shirk*.

Allah the Almighty says:

> {And proclaim to mankind the *Hajj* (pilgrimage). They will come to you on foot and on every lean camel, they will come from every deep and distant (wide) mountain highways (to perform *Hajj*). That they may witness things that are of benefit to them (i.e. reward of *Hajj* in the Hereafter, and also some worldly gain from trade, etc.), and mention the Name of Allah on appointed days (i.e. 10th, 11th, 12th, and 13th day of Dhul-Hijjah), over the beast of cattle that He has provided for them *(*for sacrifice) at the time of their slaughtering by saying: *(Bismillah, Wallahu-Akbar, Allahumma Minka* wa *Ilaik.)* Then eat thereof and feed therewith the poor who

have a very hard time. Then, let them complete the prescribed duties *(Manasik of Hajj)* for them, and perform their vows, and circumambulate the ancient House (the Ka'bah at Makkah).}
(V.22:27-29)

The holy sanctuaries must be respected:

Allah has specified some places symbolizing His honor and dignity like, Ka'bah, Arafat, Muzdalifah, Mina, As-Safa, Al-Marwah, Station of Abraham, the Sanctified Mosque, the whole of Makkah and the entire Haram. People have been inspired and blessed with an ardent desire to visit these places so that they may flock here from all the nooks and corners of the world, whether mounted on the backs of animals, or traveling on foot, they all come from afar to witness the House of Allah, bearing the hardships of journey, wearing specified unsewn clothes, reaching there in a peculiar guise and assuming a typical physiognomy, offering sacrifices in the Name of Allah, completing their vows, circumambulating the House of Allah and fulfilling their innermost aspirations towards expressing their gratitude to their Lord upon reaching there, kissing its doorsteps and making supplications to Allah by holding on to the fringes of the Ka'bah covering and thereby bursting into tears, sitting there in *I'tikaf* observing the remembrance of Allah day and night, and someone being blessed with a perfect happiness out of merely standing there with respect.[1] However, all the above things are observed to pay one's homage and tributes to Allah and to express one's honor and gratitude towards Him. Allah the Almighty becomes pleased with these activities and rewards His slaves in both this world and the Hereafter. Therefore, carrying out these activities to propitiate any other entity other than Allah is forbidden and regarded as an act of Shirk. Traveling to distant places and bearing the rigors of travel merely to visit a grave or a sanctum of a saint in tattered and dirty clothes, offering animal sacrifices upon reaching there, completing one's vows there, circumambulating someone's house or a grave, respecting the forest around it, abstaining from hunting there, not cutting trees there, not pulling out the grass and straws from there, carrying out the other similar activities and looking forward to the goodness in this world and the Hereafter (out of performing these activities) are all acts of Shirk which one must avoid. This is because we should only .hold those places in high esteem, which Shari 'ah itself has commanded us to honor as dignified ones. And showing a similar respect in relation to the places other than the specified ones according to one's own whims and inducting such novelties into religion by applying one's own domineering assumptions, are all acts of *Bid'ah* (innovation). Compliance and obedience should be observed in regard to Allah only and not the things created by Him.

Anything dedicated to an entity other than Allah is forbidden:
Allah the Almighty says:

"Say (O Muhammad {Peace be upon Him}): 'I find not in that which has been inspired to me anything forbidden to be eaten by one who wishes to eat it, unless it be *Maytatah* (a dead animal)

---

[1] The statement of Shah Shaheed lends a credence to the view that the book *Taqwiyat-ul-Iman* was written after his return from *Hajj* because this kind of detailed description is only possible after one's return from *Hajj*. This is merely our opinion and Allah knows the best.

or blood poured forth (by slaughtering or the like), or the flesh of swine (pork, etc.) for that surely is impure, or impious (unlawful) meat (of an animal) which is slaughtered as a sacrifice for other than Allah (or has been slaughtered for idols etc., or on which Allah's Name has not been mentioned while slaughtering). But whosoever is forced by necessity without willful disobedience, nor transgressing due limits, (for him) certainly, your Lord is Oft-forgiving, Most Merciful." (V.6:145)

It means that just as the flesh of swine, blood and the dead animals have been declared as forbidden ones, a slaughtered animal which has been dedicated to an entity other than Allah is also forbidden. Thus it becomes clear to us that an animal devoted and dedicated to anything created (i.e. by Allah) is forbidden and impure. For instance, an animal becomes forbidden if the same is declared as belonging to a certain person by saying "This cow belongs to Saiyid Ahmad Kabeer or this goat belongs to Sheikh Saddoo etc. etc.[1] This verse does not specify that the animal shall become forbidden only if the name of an entity other than Allah is invoked while it is being slaughtered, but the verse states that the same turns forbidden merely by the act of dedication. Any animal, whether a hen or a goat, a camel or a cow, in case dedicated to any of the creatures, be it a saint or a Prophet, a father or a grandfather, a preceptor or a fairy, is absolutely forbidden and impure, and the one who does this act is a *Mushrik* (polytheist).

Authority and command is only for Allah:

Allah the Almighty has stated the story of the Prophet Yusuf (Joseph) {Peace be upon Him} as to what he conveyed to his companions in the prison in the following words:

{O two companions of the prison! Are many different lords (gods) better or Allah, the One, the Irresistible? You do not worship besides Him but only names which you have named (forged), you and your fathers, for which Allah has sent down no authority. The command (or the judgment) is for none but Allah. He has commanded that you worship none but Him (i.e. His Monotheism), that is the (true) straight religion, but most men know not.}(V. 12:39,40)

It is painful and disgusting for a slave to have several masters. How great it is to have a single and solitary Lord who is the strongest of all! Hence, there is only one Lord who fulfills all the needs of a human being and helps him in overcoming his difficulties. The false and fictitious lords stand nowhere before Him. Nay, these are absolutely baseless fallacies to suppose that a certain deity induces rain, growing grains belongs to some other deity, blessing with children falls under someone else's jurisdiction whereas giving health is someone else's responsibility. People themselves have assigned names to them by supposing that such and such deity is responsible about such and such actions and they themselves call upon them whenever they need them and thus this practice gradually grows into an established custom in the society in due course of time.

Giving someone false and fabricated names is an act of *Shirk*:

All best and good names belong to Allah only. Who else may be called by these names other than Allah Himself? None but He Alone has these names. In case someone has this kind of names, it has nothing to do with Allah's Will. The one who is responsible about all the actions is known as

---

[1] An imaginary preceptor of women in whose name a goat is sacrificed.

Allah and the one who is known as Muhammad or Ali has no power or authority to do anything at all. Allah has not commanded us to nurse these kind of thoughts and what the creatures (i.e. people) command to do is not lawful and creditable. Allah Himself has forbidden us to maintain these kind of views. Therefore, who else other than Allah is more creditable in these matters? The pure and true religion is that one should comply with the instructions of Allah and renunciate all the other commands contradicting them. But unfortunately, the majority of people have strayed from the Right Path and have accorded priority to the ways of their preceptors, *Imam* and saints rather than following the path prescribed by Allah.

So-called customs are acts of *Shirk*:

It thus becomes clear to us that denying all the so-called customs and forged concepts and a strict adherence to the laws of Allah is a thing which Allah has determined and specified for His honor and dignity.[1] If someone treats a creature in a similar manner, he will be deemed as an absolute *Mushrik* (polytheist). The conveyance of Divine decrees and commandments to the human beings is only possible through the Messengers. If someone gives precedence to the saying of an *Imam, Mujtahid,* a *Ghauth,* a *Qutub,* a religious scholar, a preceptor, a saint, one's father or grandfather, a king, a minister, a priest or a pundit over the commandments of Islamic law or happens to prefer the ideas and methodologies devised by the preceptors and saints in an open defiance of Qur'an and *Hadith,* or nursing a persuasion in regard to the Prophets that *Shari'ah* merely consists of their own commands to the effect that they said whatever they wished to say and it became an obligation on their *Ummah* to abide by their dictates. All the above things and utterances confirm one's *Shirk*. One must firmly believe that Allah is the real ruler and has everything at His disposal and a Prophet is merely assigned to convey the Divine Commands to the people. Anything which lies within the framework of Qur'an and *Hadith* must be recognized and verified and the one which is contrary to it must be avoided.

Keeping people stand up in one's honor is prohibited:

It is reported on the authority of Mu'awiyah {May Allah have mercy on him} that Allah's Messenger {Peace be upon Him} said:

"Whosoever becomes pleased with the realization of fact that the people stand up (as a token of respect) before him like pictures (i.e. silent and immovable), let him have an abode in Hell-fire."
(Tirmidhi)

It means that whoever so desires that the people should stand up before him as a token of respect with folded hands, becoming as immobile as statues, not budging an inch, observing a pin-drop silence and not even fluttering an eyelid, such a person is bound to taste Hell-fire, for he is laying

---

[1] It means that anyone authenticating a command, custom or way of life devised by the mortals (creatures brought into existence by Allah), and thereby considering them as authoritative, commits a proven act of *Shirk*. If such a person does not seek Allah's forgiveness in earnest prior to his death, he will be doomed to burn in the Hell-fire till eternity.

a claim at Divinity and is looking forward to the kind of honor and dignity which Allah has specified for none but Himself. During a prayer, a person stands upright silently with folded hands without moving one's eyes in either direction. The posture of standing up is exclusively prescribed for the sole purpose of paying one's tributes to Allah the Almighty. Thus it becomes known to us that observing such a posture (standing up) before a person with an intention of giving him a respectful treatment is unfair and an act of *Shirk*.

Worshipping idols and the so-called "Sanctums of saints" is an act of *Shirk*:
It is reported on the authority of Thauban {May Allah have mercy on him} that Allah's Messenger {Peace be upon Him} said:

> "The Doomsday shall not be heralded until the tribes of my *Ummah* join the polytheists and practice idolatry." (Tirmidhi).

Idols are of two kinds. Erecting someone's statue or his picture and worshipping it, is called *Sanam* in Arabic. Dedicating a thing, a place, a tree, a stone, a wooden object or a paper etc. to a certain deity and then worshipping it, is known as *Wathan*. A grave, a seat of a saint, a coffin, a stick, a *Ta'zia,* a flag, a *Shaddah*[1] the *Hinna* of *Imam* Qasim and Sheikh Abdul-Qadir, a raised platform of an *Imam,* the places where the teachers and preceptors are seated, are all included in *Wathan*. It also includes a shelf in the wall, a sign or a cannon dedicated to a martyr where a goat is sacrificed, or the places attributed to some diseases and dedicated to certain deities like Satila, Masani, Bhawani, Kali, Kalka and Barahi[2] etc. The worshipping of both *Sanam* and *Wathn* confirm one's *Shirk*. The noblest of the Prophets {Peace be upon Them} prophesied that the Muslims shall be involved in this kind of Shirk just prior to the Doomsday, contrary to the other polytheists like the Hindus or the erstwhile polytheists of the Arabian Peninsula. The people of both these kinds are polytheists and the enemies of Allah and the Prophet {Peace be upon Him}.

Slaughtering an animal in a name other than that of Allah is a curse:
It is * reported on the authority of Abu Tufail {May Allah have mercy on him}that Ali {May Allah have mercy on him} took out a book which contained a *Hadith* stating that:

> "Whoever slaughtered an animal by invoking a name other than that of Allah, brings upon

---

[1] It is a flag which accompanies *Ta'ziya* commemorating the martyrs of Karbala.
[2] These are the different goddesses of the Hindus:

Satila: A goddess of smallpox. In case this epidemic breaks out, her worship is conducted as a precaution to ward off the ailment.

Masani: According to the Hindu faith, Satila had seven sisters. Masani is one of them. She was considered the goddess of chicken pox or the goddess of younger sister. Bhawani, Kali, and Kalka are also among the several goddesses of Hindus.

Barahi: The name of a goddess of diseases amont the Hindus which is worshipped and propitiated so that she may obviate the diseases.

May be someone is intrigued with a question as to why Shah Shaheed {May Allah have mercy on him}made the mention of the customs among the Hindus. The answer to this question is that the Muslims, on many occasions, adopted Hindu customs as a result of following them, a fact which he himself points out to later on.

himself the curse of Allah." (Muslim)

It means that anyone who slaughters an animal in the name of a creature (to the exclusion of Allah the Almighty) is indeed an accursed and a condemned person.

Ali {May Allah have mercy on him}had written several *Ahadith* of Allah's Messenger {Peace be upon Him} in a note-book and this *Hadith* was one of those ones. Thus it becomes known to us that an animal becomes *Halal* (permissible and lawful for the human consumption) while the same is slaughtered by invoking only Allah's Name on it. Slaughtering an animal while invoking a name other than that of Allah is an act of *Shirk* and renders an animal thus slaughtered as unlawful. Similarly an animal which is dedicated to a deity other than Allah is unlawful even if Allah's Name is invoked on it while it is being slaughtered.

Indications heralding the advent of Doomsday:

It has been narrated by Aishah {May Allah be pleased with Her} that she heard Allah's Prophet {Peace be upon Him} saying:

"The day and night shall continue to chase each other until *Al-Laat* and *Al-Uzza* (names of two idols) are not worshipped again." She asked him, "O Allah's Prophet! Since Allah has revealed the verse, 'He it is Who sent His Messenger (Muhammad {Peace be upon Him}) with guidance and the religion of truth (Islamic Monotheism) to make it victorious over all (other) religions even though the *Mushrikun* (polytheists, pagans, idolaters, and disbelievers in the Oneness of Allah and in His Messenger Muhammad {Peace be upon Him} hate (it).' I was predominantly of the view that this religion shall prevail until the end (without receding)." The Prophet {Peace be upon Him} answered that this religion shall continue to thrive with the same magnificence as long as Allah wills it to be. Then Allah will send down a blissful and chaste breeze which, (in its wake) shall take away the lives of all who even possess merely an iota of *Iman* (Faith) in their hearts. Only the bad and vice-ridden people shall be spared to exist who will revert to the religion of their fore-fathers." (Muslim)

It implies that the sense which `Aishah {May Allah have mercy on her} inferred from the verse of *Sural Al-Bara'ah (At-Taubah)* is that Islam shall prevail until the Doomsday. The Prophet {Peace be upon Him} stated that Islam's supremacy shall persist as long as Allah wills it to be. Then Allah will send down a blissful and chaste breeze which will end the lives of all those having the least amount of Faith whereas the vice-ridden and irreligious people shall be spared to live on. The hearts of these people shall be devoid of the dignity of the Prophet {Peace be upon Him}nor shall they have any interest in religion. They shall eagerly snap on the customs and rituals of their grand-fathers who were none other than the ignorant polytheists. A man who adopts the ways of the polytheists will naturally become one of them. Thus it becomes known to us that the old polytheism shall also be wide-spread during the concluding periodic phase of the world. Presently, all kinds of *Shirk* (both the ancient and new ones) are rampant among the Muslims. What the Prophet {Peace be upon Him} prophesied earlier seems to be coming true now. For instance, the Muslims are treating Prophets, saints, *Imam* and martyrs etc. polytheistically. Similarly the old polytheism also seems to be gaining ground as the Muslims deify and believe in the idols peculiarly belonging to the polytheists and follow their rituals, i.e. consulting pundits about the future events, taking something as a bad omen, believing in propitious hours (hours of happy augury to commence an event or activity), worshipping Satila and Masani, invoking the so-called deities like Hanuman, Noona[1] and Kalwa, observing the festivals of Holi, Diwali, Nauroze and Maharjan, believing in the foreboding evil of the moon entering into the zodiac of scorpion and cherishing a belief that the last few days of a lunar month (in which the moon is not visible) are ill-fated. All these myths and superstitions originally belong to the Hindus which are now rife among the Muslims. Thus it becomes known to us that the Muslims shall be indulged into committing *Shirk* in such a manner that they shall abide by the customs of their forefathers by putting aside the injunctions and teachings of Qur'an and *Hadith*.

Worshipping the places of saints is an act of the worst people:

It is narrated by Abdullah bin Umar {May Allah have mercy on him} that the Prophet {Peace be upon Him} said:

"At the advent of *Ad-Dajjal* (the Antichrist), Allah will send Jesus {Peace be upon Him}to this earth who will trace him out and do away with him. Then Allah will cause a cool breeze to blow, originating from the direction of Syria, which will take away the lives of all those who cherish even a minute particle of Faith in their hearts. Only the vice-ridden people who would be as insensible as birds and as ferocious and blood-thirsty as beasts shall be spared to live on. They will be absolutely deprived of the capability of discerning good from bad. Satan will approach them in a human guise and say to them, "Don't you feel shy?" People will enquire of him as to what he really means by it. Then he will instruct them to practice idolatry and worshipping the places. The people would then be engrossed in these acts of vice and shall be enjoying an abundant supply of their livelihood and leading a life of a perfect ease and comfort." (Muslim)

It means that during the last stage of the world's existence, the faithful will cease to exist and the unfaithful and the foolish will thrive who will have no scruples about brazenly usurping the wealth of other people. They will be totally devoid of the quality of discerning good from bad. Then Satan will appear to them in the guise of a saint and shall sermonize them by telling them that since being irreligious is a disgrace, they should turn religious. His exhortations shall eventually be heeded and the people will be rather enthused and inclined towards learning religion, but instead of following Qur'an and *Hadith*, they will be misled into concocting and fabricating what they shall presume to be as religious norms. They will do so by exercising their own judgment (banking purely on their own alleged and so called wisdom) and thus they shall be entangled into committing *Shirk* (polytheism), but they shall be awarded a further abundance in their livelihood and prosperity and shall be leading an extremely comfortable and easy life. They will be under the impression that since they are on the Right Path, Allah is pleased with them and hence they are prosperous and well-off. As a consequence, they shall be steeped into *Shirk* more and more on the pretext that the more we believe in these rituals and follow them, the more our desires get fulfilled. Therefore, a Muslim should fear Allah that He at times gives a long rope to His slaves. It does happen on many occasions that someone gets involved in *Shirk* (polytheistic

---

[1] "Luna" or 'Noona Chamari' was a famous witch of Bengal.

2. 'Nauroze' and 'Maharjan' are the festivals of Persians.
The intromission of moon into the zodiac of scorpion was considered to be a bad omen.

acts), asks the entities other than Allah to grant him his wishes, but Allah Gust for the sake of giving devil his due share), grants him his wishes. And this person erroneously believes that so long as I am on the Right Path, there -is nothing wrong in believing other deities (to the exclusion of Allah), and had it been otherwise, how could I be granted my wishes? Therefore, one must never depend on the fulfillment or non-fulfillment of one's desires and must never forsake the true religion of Allah, (due to these trifles) which is *Tauhid* (Islamic Monotheism). This *Hadith* makes it clear to us that however thick-skinned and callous a man becomes, however does he get immersed in sins, however he becomes shameless and brazenly in having no qualms about unlawfully devouring the wealth of others or in the matter of not differentiating between good and bad; he is still better than the one who commits *Shirk* and believes in the (so-called) deities to the exclusion of Allah, because the Satan instructs people to believe in these things (i.e. acts of *Shirk*) by weaning them off the above vices and depravities.[1]

Performing *Tawaf* of the idols:
It is narrated by Abu Hurairah {May Allah have mercy on him} that the Prophet {Peace be upon Him} said:

> "The Doomsday shall never be heralded until the posteriors of the women of Daus tribe do not start throbbing and wobbling around *Dhul-Khalasah* (an idol) (i.e. unless they do not circumambulate it)." (Agreed upon)

There was a certain clan among the Arabs who were known as 'Daus'. During the days of *Jahiliyah* (pre-Islamic period), they used to worship an idol which was called *Dhul-Khalasah*. During the days of the Prophet {Peace be upon Him} it was demolished. The Prophet {Peace be upon Him} made a prediction that just prior to the Doomsday, people will renew their Faith in it and the women belonging to the clan of Daus shall go around it. The Prophet {Peace be upon Him} (by dint of a clairvoyance conferred on him by Allah) sighted their posteriors shaking about to and fro (around this idol). Thus it becomes clear to us that circumambulating any place other than the House of Allah is an act of *Shirk* and a ritual peculiar to disbelievers.

---

[1] This statement aims at providing a clear idea of the utmost depravity and an extreme abomination which the polytheism involves. It never implies that "one is licensed to commit any sinful act on the condition that he refrain from practicing *Shirk* (polytheism)."

Chapter Seven
Prohibition of *Shirk* in Social Customs

This chapter contains various Verses and *Ahddith* which prove that the manner in which a man expresses his gratitude to Allah and dignifies Him in his day-to-day mundane affairs, observing and employing different modes, he must refrain from doing the same in respect of any entity other than Allah.

The whispering of Satan (Devil prodding):

Allah the Almighty says:

{They (all those who worship others than Allah) invoke nothing but female deities besides Him (Allah), and they invoke nothing but Satan a persistent rebel!" Allah cursed him. And he (Satan) said: 'I will take an appointed portion of your slaves. Verily, I will mislead them, and surely, I will arouse in them false desires; and certainly, I will order them to slit the ears of cattle, and indeed I will order them to change the nature created by Allah. And whoever takes Satan as a *Wali* (protector or helper) instead of Allah, has surely suffered a manifest loss. He (Satan) makes promises to them, and arouses in them false desires; and Satan's promises are nothing but deceptions. The dwelling of such (people) is Hell, and they will find no way of escape from it.}
(V.4:117-120)

The people who invoke deities other than Allah, they worship none but females (according to them). Someone calls upon Hazrat Bibi, someone Bibi Asiyah, someone Bibi Utawli, someone red fairy, someone black fairy, someone Satila, someone Masani and someone goddess Kali. These are merely fancies having no trace of reality. These presumed male and female deities are none but delinquent fallacies and whisperings induced by Satan which the people have taken to be the objects of worship. The one who speaks and creates spectacles (by playing tricks) sometimes, is none other than Satan himself.

All the acts of worship which are being carried out by these polytheists are to propitiate none but Satan. According to them, they only make their vows and offerings to women, but in fact it is all seized upon by Satan. These things neither benefit them in terms of religion nor help them in their mundane affairs. Since Satan himself is a renegade and an outcast, how could he possibly benefit someone in terms of his religious and moral edification? Moreover, he is a sworn enemy to the mankind and hence no favor could ever be expected from an antagonist.

He has already stated in the presence of Allah saying, "I will convert many of Your slaves into my own slaves. I shall destroy their wisdom in such a manner that they will recognize their own ideas as authentic ones and follow them. They shall dedicate animals to me which shall be bar-coded with the sign of such vows which they would be making in my name. For instance, they shall slit an animal's ears or amputate them, or they shall put a sash around it's neck, or color its forehead with henna, or embellish its face with trappings, or place a coin in its mouth. Be it as it may, any sign which denotes that this animal relates to a vow belonging to such and such deity is included in this category. Satan had already gone to the extent of saying that I shall hold such a sway on people that they shall be persuaded to deform the shapes and facial features created by

Allah. Someone shall raise a plait in someone's name, someone shall perforate his nose or ear in the name of some deity, someone shall shave off his beard and someone shall exhibit his mendicancy by shaving off his eyebrows. These are satanic deeds and are contrary to the Islamic teachings. Then the one who abandons Allah, the Munificent and follows the path of Satan, is bound to suffer a manifest loss. This is owing to the fact that first of all, Satan is an enemy to the human beings. Secondly, he is not capable of doing anything other than inducing whispering in the hearts of the people. He beguiles and placates people momentarily by making false promises to them by suggesting that if you believe in such and such deity, your such and such wishes shall be fulfilled. He allures them with tremendous aspirations that if you could muster a certain massive amount of riches, you may acquire for yourself such resplendently beautiful garden, an orchard for a magnificent palace. As long as these hopes are evanescent and never get materialized, the man gets fidgeted, forgets Allah in his spasmodic bewilderment and runs after the so-called deities. All his wild and erratic pursuits turn out to be a cry in the wilderness bearing no fruits as he acquires nothing except what has already been penned down in his destiny. This is nothing but a deceptive mirage and a whispering aroused by Satan. The outcome of all this trumpery is that a man becomes entangled and enmeshed into the quagmire of *Shirk* and deserves the Hellfire. He falls prey to the ruses of the Devil so dangerously that despite trying his might and mane, he finds himself unable (and incapacitated) to get himself freed from his tentacles.

Polytheistic rituals in regard to the soliciting of children:

Allah the Almighty says:

{It is He Who has created you from a single person (Adam), and (then) He has created from him his wife (Eve), in order that he might enjoy the pleasure of living with her. When he had sexual relation with her, she became pregnant and she carried it about lightly. Then when it became heavy, they both invoked Allah, their Lord (saying): If you give us a *Salih* child (good in every aspect), we shall indeed be among the grateful. But when He gave them a *Salih* child (good in every aspect), they ascribed partners to Him (Allah) in that which He has given to them. High is Allah, Exalted above all that they ascribe as partners to Him.} (V. 7: 189,190)

It alludes to the fact that Allah Himself created the man originally gave him a wife and caused a feeling of love to grow between them. And when they expected a child, they made supplications to Allah that they would be extremely thankful to Him if He blessed them with a *Salih* child (i.e. good in every aspect of life and robust in health and sound in his mental faculties etc.) Once blessed with such a child according to what they longed for, they turned into the devotees of the so-called deities and started making vows to them. Some people take their children to the graves of saints and some to their sanctums. Someone raises a braided plait on his shaven head in someone's name, whereas someone else either puts a sash (around one's neck)[1] or a chain (around one's neck or feet). Someone even goes to the extent of committing such an inequity that he

---

[1] A sash or chain of administering a vow People wear them at the time of making a vow, and take them off at it's completion. This is a custom observed by many people.

coerces and subjugates his child to turn into a mendicant (as a gratitude towards the accomplishment of his vow to a deity) and giving his children such polytheistic names like Nabi Bakhsh, Ali Bakhsh, Pir Bakhsh, Satila Bakhsh, Ganga Bakhsh, Jamna Das, etc. etc. As far as Allah is concerned, He is totally free from their callousness and insensitivity, but these dolts become deprived of their Faith.

Polytheistic rituals in Agriculture:

Allah the Almighty says:

{And they assign to Allah a share of the tilth and cattle which He has created, and they say: 'This is for Allah' according to their pretending and this is for our (Allah's so-called) partners.' But the share of their (Allah's so-called) 'partners' reaches not Allah, while the share of Allah reaches their (Allah's so-called) "partners!" Evil is the way they judge!} (V.6:136)

It means that even though there is no denying in the fact that all the grain and animals have been created by Allah, but despite having a cognizance of this fact, polytheists dedicate some things of theirs for the false deities other than Allah as like they dedicate for Allah and it is an astonishing reality that the tremendous amount of respect which they observe while dedicating these things to the other so-called deities, they fail to exhibit the same amount of veneration while apportioning Allah's share in their offerings.

Polytheistic rituals in regard to the cattle:

Allah the Almighty says:

{And according to their pretending, they say' such and such cattle and crops are forbidden, and none should eat of them except those whom we allow.' And (they say) there are cattle forbidden to be used for burden or any other work, and cattle on which (at slaughtering) the Name of Allah is not pronounced; lying against Him (Allah). He will recompense them for what they used to fabricate.} (V.6:138)

Some people express their opinion about a certain thing (by merely running a conjecture) that such and such thing is a unique one having a streak of oddity, and therefore it only behooves that particular person to have it. Some people do not use these animals as beasts of burden and do not let others ride them either, on the plea that as long as this animal is under a vow (made to such and such deity), it commands our respect and thus we are bound to hallow it as a sacred entity. Some people dedicate the animals to the so-called deities presuming that these acts shall go a long way to propitiate Allah and thus their long-cherished penchants shall be fulfilled, but fallacious are their conjectures and deeds for which shall they indeed be penalized.

Allah the Almighty says:

{Allah has not instituted things like *Bahirah* (a she-camel whose milk was spared for the idols and nobody was allowed to milk it) or a *Saibah* (a she-camel let loose for free pasture for their false gods, e.g. idols, etc. and nothing was allowed to be carried on it), or a *Wasilah* (a she-camel at it's first delivery and then again gives birth to a she camel at it's second delivery) or a *Ham* (a stallion-camel freed from work for their idols, after it had finished a number of copulations assigned for it, all these animals were liberated in honor of idols as practiced by pagan Arabs in the pre-Islamic period). But those who disbelieve invent lies against Allah, and most of them have no understanding.} (V.5:l03)

A ritual slit was used to be etched out on to the ear of an animal which was dedicated to a certain deity. This kind of animal was known as *Bahirah*. Had this animal been a bull, it was called *Sdibah*.. An animal which was declared to be under such a conditional vow that if the same gave birth to a male colt, it (the colt) would be given away as an offering. Now, if the said animal gave birth to both a male and female offspring at one stroke, they would refrain from giving away even the male colt as an offering. Such a pair of colts was called *Wasilah*. People would stop riding and putting their burden on an animal which gave birth to ten off-springs. Such an animal was called *Ham*. It has clearly been stated that all these practices are merely customs and rituals and have nothing to do with the injunctions of *Shari 'ah*.

Thus it becomes known to us that the acts of dedicating an animal to a certain deity, bar-coding it, and determining that such and such deity shall only accept a cow, a goat or a hen in terms of offerings (against vows made to them), are nothing but the myths and rituals of ignorance and are in contravention of the sanctified Islamic law.

Slandering Allah in the matters of lawful and forbidden things:

Allah the Almighty says:

{And say not concerning that which your tongues put forth falsely: 'This is lawful and this is forbidden,' so as to invent lies against Allah. Verily, those who invent lies against Allah will never prosper.}(V.16:ll6)

It means that one should not take it upon himself to determine as to what is lawful and what isn't, because such an act is the sole prerogative of Allah. This sort of thing shall only amount to inventing lies against Allah. It is wrong to be driven by one's own flights of fancies that if that particular assignment is undertaken after this particular fashion, it will click or else it shall go haywire, for one can never succeed by inventing lies against Allah. Thus it becomes known to us that fostering such myths that one should not partake of betel leaves in the month of Muharram, one should not wear red dresses, the male should not eat the food of vowing in the name of Bibi, a food offering made in the name of a certain saint must contain those particular vegetables or the same should necessary contain *Missi* (a kind of female cosmetics in the olden days) and henna etc., or declaring that such a food should not be eaten by a female slave or for the woman who remarries (either after the death of her first husband or after being divorced by him) or the ones belonging to the lower castes of the society, or an adulteress, declaring that the offering made in the name of Shah Abdul-Haque (a saint) has to be a *Halwa* (a sweet dish) necessarily which should be prepared with an utmost precaution and that it should not be had by someone who is addicted to using a hubble-bubble, alleging that the offering made to Shah Madar (a saint) has to be *Maleeda* (a sweet dish); the one offered to Bu Ali Qalandar, has to be a dish of *Siwaiyan* (vermicelli) and the one offered in the name of the Companions of the Cave *(Ashdbe-Kahf)*, a dish of meat and bread. Giving currency to such myths that on the occasion of someone's marriage or in the event of somebody's death, it is necessary to observe such and such customs, propagating such ideas that a woman should not remarry after the death of her husband, should not attend a marriage ceremony or should not marinate pickles, fanning a superstition that this particular person should not wear blue clothes and that person should abstain himself from wearing red ones etc. All the above things are acts of *Shirk* and the people who perpetrate such things are in fact interfering in the matters which solely belong to Allah the Almighty and hence are inventing their own *Shari' ah*.

Giving credit to the influence of planets (Zodiac signs), is an act of *Shirk*:

Zaid bin Khalid bin Juhni {May Allah have mercy on him} narrated the following *Hadith:*

> "One day the Prophet {Peace be upon Him} led us the morning prayer in Hudaibiyah pursuant to a night-long rain. After completing the prayer, he diverted his attention to the people and said, 'Do you know what your *Rabb* said?' The Companions {May Allah be pleased with Them} answered that Allah and His Prophet {Peace be upon Him} knew the best. The Prophet {Peace be upon Him} answered, 'Allah said that among the slaves of mine who entered the morning, some were believers and some disbelievers. The one who said that this rain was induced due to the blessing and mercy of Allah has indeed affirmed his Faith in Me and denounced the stars and the one who said that this rain was caused and brought by such and such star[1], has denounced me and affirmed his Faith in stars." (Al-Bukhari -Muslim)

It means that the one who cherishes such a belief that the stars (which are merely a creation of Allah) exercise their influence in the matters of the universe, Allah considers him as the one who negates Him. Such a person is none but a star-worshipper. The one who affirms that this universe is operative by Allah's command, is His beloved slave and not a star-worshipper. Thus, we understand that believing in propitious and unpropitious hours, making an inquiry as to which day or date is auspicious or inauspicious (to commence an activity) and giving one's credit to the observations of an astrologer are the activities which open the door to *Shirk* (polytheism). This is due to the fact that all these activities belong to astrology and these are only the star-worshippers who believe in them.

The astrologers are magicians and the magicians are disbelievers:

It is narrated by Ibn Abbas{May Allah have mercy on him} that the Prophet {Peace be upon Him} said:

> "The one who learns a chapter of astrology in a way contrary to the commandments of Allah, has

---

[1] 'Naw' is translated as 'Zodiac'. It implies one's destiny, fate, horoscope or a certain position within the constellation. The expression implies the position of the moon in the sky.

In the terminology of astrology, it implies those planets or the zodiac positions of the moon which are in a swinging motion day and night. They are attributed to be carrying special effects and specific modes of influence on each hour of the day and night. Astrologers pronounce something as auspicious or in auspicious by observing them, which is absolutely wrong.

learnt a part of magic. An astrologer is a soothsayer, a soothsayer is a magician, and a magician is a disbeliever." (Razin)[1]

It means that the Noble Qur'an states that the stars are a manifestation of the power and wisdom of Allah. They serve as an embellishment to the sky and a scourge to drive away the Devil.[2] The Qur'an never states that these stars have the power to interfere in the running of nature or that they have a direct bearing on the virtuosity and vices taking place in the world.

Now, if someone disregards the former merits of the stars and postulates that these heavenly bodies influence the worldly affairs and thus claims to have the knowledge of the unseen, he indeed is a polytheist. As the soothsayers, in the pre-Islamic period of ignorance, used to predict about the unseen by consulting the jinns, the astrologers do the same by consulting the stars which means that a soothsayer, an astronomer, a *Rammal* (a conjurer), a *Jaffar* (a soothsayer) all follow the same creed. A *Kahin* (the one who prophesies about the future events) courts friendship with the jinns just like a magician and the same is not possible until one believes in them, invokes them and makes an offer to them. It all relates to infidelity and making partners to Allah. May Allah the Almighty save and preserve Muslims from committing acts or *Shirk. Amin.*

The Sin of believing in Astrology:

It is narrated by Hafsah {May Allah have mercy on Her} the Mother of Believers, that the Prophet {Peace be upon Him} said:

> "The one who approaches a soothsayer and consults him about any matter, his prayers shall not be accepted for forty days." (Muslim)

It means that anybody who approaches a certain person, claiming to have the knowledge of the unseen, and thus enquires of him about any of his problems, his prayers shall not be accepted for forty days. This is due to the fact that such a person has committed an act of *Shirk,* and *Shirk* destroys all acts of worship. An astrologer, a conjurer, a diviner, the one who predicts about the unseen by casting lots etc. are all categorized as soothsayers.

Deducing an Omen is an act of disbelief:

It is narrated by Qabisah {May Allah have mercy on him} that the Prophet {Peace be upon Him} said:

> "The acts of making prophesies through making a bird fly, or casting lots to infer a good or bad omen or declaring something to be carrying a foreboding presentiment are acts of disbelief and

---

[1] Razin bin Mu'awiyah is one of the leading narrators of *Hadith*. He died in the sixth century according to the *Hijra* calendar.

[2] The three advantages of stars which are mentioned in the Noble Qur'an are: Beautification of sky, driving away the devils and providing guidelines to the sea and land travelers.

apostasy."[1]

It is narrated by Abdullah bin Mas'ud {May Allah have mercy on him} that the Prophet {Peace be upon Him} said:

"Taking an omen is an act of *Shirk*, taking an omen is an act of *Shirk*, taking an omen is an act of *Shirk!*"

The custom of taking an omen was rife in the Arabian society and the Arabs had a great belief in it. The Prophet {Peace be upon Him} reiterated that it is an act of *Shirk* so that the people should refrain from having a faith in this absurdity.

Sa'd bin Malik {May Allah have mercy on him} narrated that the Prophet {Peace be upon Him} said:

"A belief (i.e. in the magical properties) that an owl is a sign of omen, is baseless, no disease gets transmitted from one person to another; and nothing is inauspicious (carries a misfortune). Had it been so, the same would have been found in a woman, a house and in a horse." (Abu Dawud)

A belief was rife among the then Arabs, about a victim of a murder whose death is still ur1fetaliated, that an owl comes out of his skull and pleads for his revenge. This owl was known as *Hammah*. The Prophet {Peace be upon Him} declared this kind of faith to be baseless. Thus, the concept of the transmigration of souls is thoroughly baseless too. The Arabs were of the opinion that the diseases like itching and leprosy etc. are contagious ones. The Prophet {Peace be upon Him} refuted this view to be an erroneous one.

Thus it becomes known to us that a view which is generally held by the people to the effect that the people suffering from smallpox should be avoided and that the children should not be permitted to go near them, is among the myths cherished by the disbelievers, and hence we should not give our credit to them, which means that we should not nurse such a faith that the ailment of that person shall strike us automatically Without the will of Allah since no disease strikes anyone unless Allah commands it to be so. (However, from the medical point of view, there is no harm in taking the necessary precautions).

A myth which has gained a wide currency among the people is that they often keep observing that

---

[1] Al-*'Iyafah* used to release a deer or a bird. If these animals proceeded to the right, they considered it to be auspicious, but if the same proceeded to the left, they considered it to be as a foreboding one and thus refrained from commencing an act. *At-Tayarah* also implies the same meaning. The people who were known as *At-Tarq* used to either cast pebbles on the ground or draw lines in the sand thereby inferring good or bad omens.

a certain assignment is inauspicious for the particular person and hence he did not succeed in it. This belief is erroneous too. The Prophet {Peace be upon Him} stated that, had something been inauspicious, it would have been a house, a horse and a woman.[1] The above things sometimes do prove to be inauspicious, but no formula has been prescribed to ascertain their inauspiciousness. A belief widespread among the people is that a house resembling a lion's mouth[2] a horse having a star-like forehead and a woman having a vicious mouth are inauspicious. These myths are baseless, having no authenticity, and the Muslims should pay no attention to them. If someone buys a new house, a horse or marries a woman, one should only ask Allah to make them auspicious for him and similarly one should seek Allah's protection from their evil. As to the rest of things, one should refrain from harboring such notions as to this particular work augured well for him whereas that particular assignment proved to be ill-starred to him, and therefore he flopped in it.

It is narrated by Abu Hurairah {May Allah have mercy on him} that the Prophet {Peace be upon Him} said:

"There is no contagion (a disease transmitting from one person to another), no owl (believing in its so-called magical properties) and no *Safar* (a ghost allegedly inhabiting the belly of a person)." (Bukhari)

A view which was rife among the Arabs regarding the people suffering from *Ju'ul-Kalb* (an ailment characterized by an insatiable hunger) was that his belly was inhabited by an evil spirit which in took all the food he devoured and therefore his hunger was never satiated. This so-called evil spirit was known as *Safar*. The Prophet {Peace be upon Him} declared that there is no such thing as a ghost or an evil-spirit (i.e. inhabiting the belly of the sick person) and this was merely a superstition. Thus we understand that the ailments are not induced by the evil spirits. Some people believe that some of the diseases occur due to the influence of some evil spirits like Satila, Masani, Barahi[3] etc. but this is untrue. During the pre-Islamic period, people used to consider the

---

[1] The Prophet {Peace be upon Him} on another occasion, elaborated on it this way:

"An evil house is the one which has bad neighbors, an evil woman is the one who is short-tempered and ill-mannered, and a horse which is not worth keeping is the one who is unruly and skittish."

[2] A house which is broad and wide at the front and small and constrained at the rear is called *Sher Dahan* (lion-mouthed). The Indians considered this type of house to be evil and inauspicious.

[3] Barahi is the name of a goddess of diseases among the Hindus, which is worshipped to repel diseases.

month of Safar as an evil one and did not perform any activity during this month. This was wrong too. Thus, it becomes known to us that considering the thirteen days of Safar as inauspicious and believing that the calamities befall the earth during this specific period and deeming a thing, date, day or an hour to be of an evil presentiment are all polytheistic concepts. It has been narrated by Ibn Majah on the authority of Jabir {May Allah have mercy on him} that the Prophet {Peace be upon Him} took the hand of a leper, put his hand along with his own hand in a bowl and said:

> "Have an absolute Faith and trust in Allah and eat."

It means that our trust lies in Allah Alone. He can inflict disease on anyone whomsoever He wishes and can make anyone hale and hearty. We, on our part, do not desist from eating with anyone and do not believe that a disease may be transmitted from one person to another.

Do not make Allah an Intercessor:

It is narrated by Abu Dawud on the authority of Jubair bin Mut'im {May Allah have mercy on him} that a nomad Arab came to the Prophet {Peace be upon Him} and said:

> "People are suffering from hardships, the children are suffering from an extreme hunger and the livestock has perished. We would like you to make supplications to Allah on our behalf to invoke rain. We would like to appoint you as our intercessor towards Allah and appoint Allah as our intercessor before you." The Prophet {Peace be upon Him} (upon hearing this) started mentioning the glory of Allah by repeating the phrase "Glory is to Allah, Glory is to Allah." He kept doing it for such a length of time that one could notice it (the expressions of curiosity) writ large on the faces of his Companions. Then the Prophet {Peace be upon Him} said, 'You the one who do not understand!' Allah does not intercede on anyone's behalf. Far Exalted is He (in his position and status) than doing this. O ignorant person! Do you know what Allah is? His Throne rests like this on the heavens!" He then made a gesture with folding his fingers in a round and convex shape denoting it to be like a dome and said that the Throne, under the weight of His Majesty is wobbling and shaking about exactly as if the saddle of a camel gyrates and creaks about under the weight of a rider."

The incident goes that once there was a drought in the Arabian Peninsula. A bedouin came to the Prophet {Peace be upon Him} and told him the sufferings of the people and asked him to make supplications to Allah. He further said that we would like to intercede with Allah on our behalf and similarly we would like Allah to be our mediator to you in this matter. Once the Prophet {Peace be upon Him} heard what he said, he started trembling due to fear of Allah and started uttering the words of praises manifesting the greatness of Allah. The facial expressions of the audience changed considerably as they heard the words epitomizing Allah's dignity and magnificence. Then the Prophet {Peace be upon Him} went on to explain to the bedouin that the authority belongs only to the Master. If the Master does the needful by accepting someone's mediation, it is so kind of him. If someone says that we have brought Allah to the Messenger as an intercessor, it means that such a person has vested an absolute power and authority in the hands of the Prophet, even though this prerogative belongs to none but Allah only. The Prophet {Peace be upon Him} enjoined upon him to never repeat like this. Allah the Almighty is so great and magnificent that all the Prophets and saints do not even measure a particle before Him. His Throne encircles all the heavens and earth just like a dome. Even though the Throne is too massive and gigantic, yet it is unable to withstand the greatness of this Emperor of emperors and thus it is wavering and creaking about. His creatures are unable to perceive and appreciate His greatness and they are not capable of expressing about it by using their normal thoughts and perceptions. Interfering in His work and laying hands in the matters concerning His great empire is out of question. He is so powerful that He can accomplish millions of things without the help of an army, or even a minister or a consultant, just in one stroke. Why should He go to anyone to intercede on someone's behalf? Who could be powerful before Him? Prophet Muhammad {Peace be upon Him}, who is the best creation of Allah among all the human beings, became flabbergasted with, consternation upon hearing an indecent remark from a bedouin and started praising Allah in every respect of His grandeur which fills the earth and the skies. What do we make out of the people who stat1 associating familiarity with Allah akin to a brother's or a friend's relationship and keep blurting out their gossips with a big mouth?

Someone says that he has purchased Allah for a mere pittance and someone alleges that he is two years older than his Lord! Someone does not even feel shy to utter a blasphemy to the effect that he would never see his Lord if He appears to him in any shape other than that of his religious preceptor. Someone has uttered a couplet which runs in the following manner:

"My heart is bruised with an extreme love of Prophet Muhammad {Peace be upon Him} and I nurse an envy against my Lord."

Another poet says:

"One must treat Allah with a madness whereas Prophet Muhammad {Peace be upon Him} must be treated with an absolute seriousness and mental composure."

Someone considers the personality of Muhammad {Peace be upon Him} preferable to Allah Himself. All these things are pathetic and utterly deplorable. Why have the Muslims turned mentally decrepit ones and have become blindfolded in the presence of the Noble Qur'an. May Allah protect us from these acts of delinquencies. *Amin.*

Someone has justifiably remarked:

"We ask Allah's guidance that may He bless us with (an attitude of) respectfulness as a disrespectful person becomes deprived of the blessing of his Lord."

A practice which is prevalent among the people is that once they conduct a gathering and complete all the portions of the Noble Qur'an therein, they pronounce a formula sentence which goes like this:
"O Sheikh Abdul Qadir Jilani! Please fulfill our desire for Allah's sake!"

This statement is a manifest *Shirk.*[1] May Allah save Muslims from such acts! One should never utter a word from his mouth which reeks of *Shirk* (polytheism) or a word which borders on impropriety and disrespectfulness towards Allah! Allah the Almighty is magnificent! He is the Emperor of emperors, Who is perfect in all respects and His glory never fades! It is only to punish one for a minor fault and forgive other for a minor deed-depends wholly on His own will. It is an arrogance to suppose that even though one has apparently used a word showing disrespectfulness, but in fact the same alludes to a distant meaning. This is due to the fact that Allah is far above it all and defies all the enigmas. If someone starts gossiping freely with his elders, it is bound to be regarded as an arrogance and sauciness. It only suits to be free with one's close friends in this respect and not with one's father or a king.

The dearest names to Allah:

It is narrated by Muslim on the authority of Ibn Umar {May Allah have mercy on him} that the Prophet said:

"The dearest names with Allah are Abdullah and Abdur-Rahman."

How lovely it is to have a name like the slave of Allah or the slave of the Most Gracious. This category includes Abdul-Quddus, Abdul-Jaleel, Abdul-Khaliq, Ilahi Bakhsh, Allah Diya, Allah Dad etc. All these names demonstrate a relationship to Allah.

Kunya [2] **(pet name) with the name of Allah must be avoided:**

It is narrated by Abu Dawud and An-Nasa'i on the authority of Shuraih bin Hani {May Allah have mercy on him}:

"When I, along with the delegation of my clan, visited the Prophet {Peace be upon Him}, he {Peace be upon Him} noticed that the people of my clan were addressing me with a patronymic appellation of *Abul-Hakam*. He (the Prophet {Peace be upon Him} called me and said, *"Hakam* (the one having a jurisdiction) is none but Allah Himself. Only His commandments are effective. Why do you have such a pet name as *Abul-Hakam."*

---

[1] According to the *Hadith* of the Prophet {Peace be upon Him}, the recitation of *Salam* on the Prophet {Peace be upon Him} prior to a supplication and after it, is the reason for the acceptance of one's supplication. Adopting someone as an intermediary (or as a means of directing one's supplications to Allah) is a practice which is not endorsed and authenticated in a fare and square manner by either of the four *Imam* or the eminent personalities of the three ages of Islam (the ages of the preferential order according to the Prophet {Peace be upon Him}. Therefore, one should also avoid resorting to such means.

[2] Calling one, "O father of so-and-so" or "a mother of so-and-so."

It means that it is only the prerogative of Allah to settle the disputes and give verdict in regard to all the dissensions, a fact which shall be demonstrated on the Day of Judgment. No other is capable of doing that. Thus it becomes clear to us that a word which only befits the magnificence of Allah must not be used for someone else. For instance, none but Allah should be called the "King of kings." "He Alone is the *Rabb* of the whole universe and can do anything He likes." This type of expressions may only be used for Allah. Similarly the expressions like the object of worship, the All-wise, the Carefree etc. are only fit to be used for Allah Alone.

Only say *Ma Shii Allah* (What Allah wished):
It is narrated in *Sharh As-Sunnah* by Hudhaifa{May Allah have mercy on him} that the Prophet {Peace be upon Him} said:

"Do not say, what Allah and Muhammad {Peace be upon Him} wished, but you should only say, what Allah wished."

It means that none of the creatures has a say in the matters concerning Divinity, no matter how great and close one that creature could be. For instance, one should never say that if Allah and His Messenger wished, it should happen so, since all the things in the world happen by the Will of Allah only and not by the will of the Prophet. If someone enquires of you as to what a person really conceals in his heart, or when that person shall be marrying or how many leaves that particular tree bears or how many stars are there up in the heavens, never respond to him by saying that these things are only known by Allah and His Prophet, as the knowledge of the unseen rests with Allah and not with His Prophet. However, there is no harm if someone says such a thing in regard to the religious matters as Allah has given a full knowledge of religion to His Prophet and has commanded people to comply with the instructions of His Prophet.

Taking an oath in the name of anyone other than Allah is an act of *Shirk*:
It is narrated by Tirmidhi on the authority of Ibn Umar {May Allah have mercy on him} that he heard the Prophet {Peace be upon Him} saying:

"The one who administers an oath in the name of anyone other than Allah, has committed an act of *Shirk.*"

It is narrated by Abdur-Rahmiin bin Samurah {May Allah have mercy on him} that the Prophet {Peace be upon Him} said:

"Do not take an oath in the name of the idols nor in the name of your fathers." (Muslim).

It is narrated by Ibn Umar {May Allah have mercy on him} that Allah's Prophet {Peace be upon Him} said:

"Allah prohibits you from taking an oath in the name of your forefathers. If anyone of you were to take an oath, let him either do it in the Name of Allah or he should observe silence." (Al-Bukhari-Muslim)

It is narrated by Abu Hurairah {May Allah have mercy on him} that the Prophet {Peace be upon Him} said:

"Whoever has taken an oath in the name of *Al-Laat* and *Al-Uzza* (name of two idols) (by the force of habit), he must say *La Ilaha ill-Allah*. (There is no one worthy of being worshipped but Allah). (Al-Bukhari-Muslim)

During the pre-Islamic period, it was a common practice to swear to the idols. After embracing Islam, if someone happens to swear to an idol unconsciously (by the force of habit), he must immediately recite *La Ilaha ill-Allah* to affirm the Oneness of Allah. Thus it becomes known to us that we must refrain from taking an oath in anyone's name other than Allah. If such a thing happens inadvertently, one must immediately seek Allah's forgiveness. The types of oaths prevalent among the polytheists tend to weaken and jeopardize the Faith.

The verdict of the Prophet {Peace be upon Him} about observing vows:

It is narrated by Thabit bin Dahhak {May Allah have mercy on him}:

A certain person during the era of the Prophet {Peace be upon Him} made a vow that he would slaughter a camel in a place known as "Bawanah." Then this person came to the Prophet {Peace be upon Him} and informed him about his vow. The Prophet {Peace be upon Him} said: Does the said place comprise any of the sanctums (dedicated to any of the deities during the pre-Islamic period)?" The Companions of the Prophet {Peace be upon Him} answered in negative. Then the Prophet enquired of them as to whether had there been any festival observed there? They still answered in negative. Then the Prophet instructed this person to go ahead with observing his vow saying that it is forbidden to observe only that kind of vow which defies and contradicts Allah's injunctions. (Abu-Dawud)

Thus it becomes known to us that it is a sinful act to observe a vow in the name of anyone other than Allah. One should never accomplish such a vow because making an intention to undertake such a vow is itself a sin and if someone still goes ahead and completes it, he will only incur an increased amount of sin. It is further added to our knowledge that a place where the animals are sacrificed in the name of the deities (to the exclusion of Allah), their worship is regularly conducted and congregational activities of *Shirk* are performed, we should not even carry there an animal which is to be sacrificed in the Name of Allah. We should also refrain from attending such activities, irrespective of our intention whether good or bad, because participating in these activities is itself a perpetually bad thing.

Prostration to Allah and paying due respect to a Messenger:

It is narrated by Aishah {May Allah have mercy on Her}:

> The Prophet {Peace be upon Him} was sitting with a group of *Muhajirin* and *Ansar*. A camel came walking all the way to the Prophet {Peace be upon Him} and prostrated before him. Upon observing this spectacle, his Companions said: "O Allah's Messenger {Peace be upon Him}! The animals and trees prostrate before you! And as long as they do it, we are more rightful in doing this to you (i.e. to prostrate before you)." The Prophet {Peace be upon Him} answered: "You must worship your Lord and pay due respect to your brothers." *(Musnad Ahmad).*

It means that all the human beings are brothers to one another. The one who is the most elderly and the most pious is an elder brother. We should respect such a person just like our elder brother. Allah is the *Rabb* of all and therefore, we should worship none but Him alone. Thus we understand that all the people who are close to Allah, regardless of whether they are Messengers or saints, are none but the helpless slaves of Allah, and are our brothers, and as long as Allah has bestowed on them marks of greatness, they are like our brothers and we are instructed to obey them. Since we are younger to them, we are instructed to respect them in their capacity as human beings only without giving them a Divine status (i.e. without making them an object of worship). It is further added to our knowledge that some saints are held in great reverence by animals and trees also and hence we do find some *Dargah* (sanctums and tombs of saints) being frequented by lions, or elephants or wolves, but the human beings are not supposed to emulate their examples and ape them in their actions. A human being may only respect someone within the limits prescribed by Allah and may not exceed it. For example, the statutes of *Shari'ah* do not permit anyone to take a residence in a tomb or around a grave in the capacity of a *Mujawir* (caretaker or custodian of a grave) and therefore, one must never become a *Mujawir* even though one may notice the presence of a lion day and night at a certain tomb of a saint, since it is not the becoming of a man to ape an animal.

It is reported by Abu Dawud on the authority of Qais bin Sa'd {May Allah have mercy on him}:

> I went to the city of Hirah where I saw the people prostrating to their king. I thought within my heart that Allah's Messenger{Peace be upon Him} indeed is more eligible and rightful to be prostrated. Therefore, I went to the Prophet {Peace be upon Him} and said: "I have seen people prostrating to their king in the city of Hira and hence you are more rightful and eligible that we should offer our prostrations to you." The Prophet {Peace be upon Him} answered: "If you happen to pass by my grave, will you still prostrate before it?" I said, "No." At this the Prophet {Peace be upon Him} said: "Then you must not do this too!"

By this the Prophet {Peace be upon Him} meant to convey it to the people that the day would come when he {Peace be upon Him} would pass away and have an eternal sleep in the grave and then he {Peace be upon Him} would not be worthy of such prostrations. The only one, worthy of prostrations, is the One Who is Eternal and Everlasting. Thus we understand that no one, whether dead or alive is eligible for prostrations. It is not permissible for one to prostrate either before a grave or at the tomb/sanctuary of a saint, because the one who is alive is definitely going to die tomorrow and the one who is dead now, had once been alive and was none but a human being. Therefore, he is still a slave of Allah after his death and has not acquired a Divine status.

It is not permissible to call someone one's slave:

It is reported by Muslim on the authority of Abu Hurairah {May Allah have mercy on him} that the Prophet {Peace be upon Him} said:

"Everyone must refrain from uttering such words like 'my male slave' or 'my female slave.' All of you are the slaves of Allah and all your women are slaves of Allah. A slave should not address his master as his lord because the Lord of you all is Allah."

Thus it becomes known to us that even the slaves, while talking to each other, must avoid such expressions during the course of their conversation such as "I am a slave of such and such person and such and such person is my lord." Taking this into consideration, how unfair is it to be known by such names (denoting slavery to someone) as the slave of the Prophet, the slave of Ali, the slave of His Excellency, the choicest worshipper, the worshipper of an adolescent boy, the worshipper of a woman, the worshipper of one's religious preceptor and what an arrogance it is to often observe such remarks that "You are the master of our lives and wealth, or we are at your absolute command, and we shall obey you in whatever you instruct us to do." All these observations are based on falsehood and *Shirk* (polytheism).

An excellent example to pay respect to the Prophet {Peace be upon Him}:

It is narrated by Umar {May Allah have mercy on him} that the Prophet {Peace be upon Him} said:

"Do not exceed the limits in dignifying me as the Christians have done to Jesus {Peace be upon Him}.I am none but Allah's slave only and therefore you should call me a slave of Allah and His Messenger." (Al-Bukhari-Muslim)

What the Prophet {Peace be upon Him} meant to convey to the people is that whatever qualities and perfections Allah has conferred on him, become epitomized in calling him a slave and a Messenger of Allah, because what greater status or title of honor may be conferred on a human being than awarding him the honor of being a Prophet? The rest of the other titles just rank underneath it. But a human being, despite being awarded Prophethood, is still a human being. He takes pride in being a slave itself. He does not acquire Divine qualities after being awarded the Prophethood and he does not get merged with Allah's Self (i.e. by losing his separate identity as a slave). We must treat human beings in their capacity of human beings only. We should not become like Christians who did not recognize Jesus {Peace be upon Him} as a human being and gave him a Divine status and thus they became disbelievers and polytheists and deserved Allah's wrath and perdition. This is the reason why the Prophet {Peace be upon Him} instructed his *Ummah* not to resort to such casuistry as done by the Christians and not to exceed the limits in lavishing undue praise to him lest it *(Ummah)* should deserve and invoke the anger of Allah on itself. But it is a deplorable fact that the rude and disrespectful people among this *Ummah* paid no heed to the instructions of the Prophet {Peace be upon Him} and started pursuing the misleading sophistry as done earlier by the Christians. The view which the Christians hold about the Jesus Christ {Peace be upon Him} is that Allah, Himself appeared assuming a guise or incarnation of Jesus Christ and therefore, Jesus Christ is a human being on one hand whereas on the other hand, he is the *Rabb*. Some supercilious and arrogant delinquents have observed exactly the same view in regard to the Prophet {Peace be upon Him} by saying:

> "The *Rabb* Himself descended this earth assuming different incarnations of the Prophets during different ages. Finally, He came down in the guise of an Arab and became the Emperor of the world."

Another poet observes:

> "You (the Prophet {Peace be upon Him}) are both a mortal and an eternal entity at the same time and your existence involves an element of possibility as well as an element of compulsion."

These kind of polytheistic expressions are intolerably repulsive and hence an abomination to the earth as well as to the heavens. May Allah award proper understanding of Faith to the Muslims. *Amin.*

Some of the unscrupulous perverts also had the cheek of fabricating a *Hadith* and ascribing it to the Prophet {Peace be upon Him} himself. According to this fabricated *Hadith,* the Prophet {Peace be upon Him} observes:

"I am Ahmad without the alphabet *"Meem"* which means that I am *Ahad* (i.e. the one and solitary, which is one of the Attributes of Allah, may Allah forbid!). Similarly, some people concocted lengthy patches of prose in Arabic, named it *Khutbat-ul-Iftikhar* and ascribed it to Ali {May Allah have mercy on him} This is a monstrous act of slandering. (O *Rabb!* You are free from all kinds of *Shirk*. This is a mighty calumnious accusation which they have directed against You. O *Rabb!* We hereby implore You to make the truth prevail over falsehood and let the perpetrators of falsehood face an ignominy in this world! *Amin.*

The Christians believe in such a faith that the Prophet Jesus Christ {Peace be upon Him} wields a jurisdiction over both the worlds. Anyone claiming to have a faith in him, if pleads him in earnest, needs not worship Allah. Sins do not affect his faith. Making a discrimination between the permissible and the forbidden does not hold true for him anymore. In another words, he is free to run berserk like a mad elephant, liberated and unfettered, and doing everything according to the dictates of his whims. He musters this audacity encouraged by the belief that Jesus Christ shall intercede with Allah on his behalf and save him from Allah's punishment. The ignorant Muslims nurse an identical belief not only in regard to the Prophet {Peace be upon Him} alone, but also in regard to every *Imam,* pious person, and preceptor. May Allah direct them to the Right Path.

It is narrated by Mutarrif bin Abdullah bin Ash-Shikhkhir {May Allah have mercy on him}that he, along with a delegation of Banu Amir tribesmen, went to Allah's Messenger {Peace be upon Him} They said:

> "You are our Lord!" The Prophet answered, "Allah is the Lord." They said, "You are superior to us, elder than us and more generous than we are." The Prophet answered, "Yes, you can say all or some of these things about me, but I am afraid lest the Devil should make you arrogant."

It means that one should observe an extreme precaution while passing a remark about a saint. One should praise a saint in his capacity as a human being only and that too within reasonable limits (i.e. avoiding exaggerations). Do not extol him to the skies lest you should commit a sacrilege towards Divinity.

The word *Saiyid* carries two meanings:

The word *Saiyid* carries two meanings which are as follows:
a) Self-dependent or independent, the master of all who is not governed by anyone, and does anything he wills to do. No one except Allah possesses this quality and magnificence and hence there is no *Saiyid* but Allah in this sense of the meaning.
b) In another sense, it implies a person who receives the instructions of a lord and then conveys it to the others. This type of sense includes a chieftain and a land-lord etc. According to this sense, each Messenger of Allah is the chief of his *Ummah,* each *Imam* a chief of his contemporaries, every *Mujtahid* a chief of his followers, every saint a chief of his devotees and every scholar a chief of his disciples. They are accorded this position of prominence due to the fact that at first, they act upon the Divine injunctions by themselves, and then they educate and instruct their youngsters in this faculty of knowledge. In this respect, our favorite and beloved Prophet {Peace be upon Him} is the *Saiyid* of the whole world. He {Peace be upon Him} has the greatest and the most exalted status with Allah. He {Peace be upon Him} was the one who followed the injunctions of *Shari'ah* to the core more than anyone else. The people stand in dire need of him to be enlightened about the religion of Allah. Therefore, He {Peace be upon Him} may semantically be called the master of the entire world, nay, we should justifiably call him so. In terms of the first implied meaning, we shouldn't even consider him {Peace be upon Him} a master of an ant, because he himself is not empowered to exercise an authority even over an ant.

Sayings of the Prophet {Peace be upon Him} in regard to the pictures:

Aishah {May Allah have mercy on Her} narrated:

"Once I bought a cushion which was decorated with pictures. When Allah's Prophet {Peace be upon Him} sighted it, he kept standing at the door and did not enter the house. I detected an expression of disgust on his face. Upon noticing it said, "O Allah's Messenger, I seek forgiveness of Allah! What have I done wrong?" The Prophet {Peace be upon Him} said: "What this cushion is all about?" I said, "I have bought it for you so that you may sit on it and use it as a pillow." The Prophet said, "The people who portray these pictures shall be subjected to a perdition on the Day of Judgment as they shall be asked to revive the picture they have portrayed." The {Peace be upon Him} further elaborated saying that the angels do not enter a house which contain pictures. (Al-Bukhari)

Since the majority of the polytheists indulge in an act of worshipping idols, the angels and the Prophets are averse to them and therefore angels do not enter such a house. The artists who portray and paint pictures shall be brought to books as they purvey to the people the paraphernalia of idolatry. It thus becomes understood that the preservation and portrayal of a picture, whether it be of a Prophet, an *Imam,* a saint, a *Qutub,* a preceptor or a devotee, is forbidden. The people who honor the portraits of their elderly folks or religious mentors and preserve them as an object of consecration are indeed the ones who have gone astray and have turned into polytheists.

Such people are abhorred by the Prophets and angels. It is an obligation on a Muslim that he must eliminate pictures of all kinds from his house considering them abominable so that the angels bearing the mercy of Allah may also enter his house thereby filling it with the element of *Barakah* (blessing).

The five major sins:

It is narrated by Ibn Abbas {May Allah have mercy on him} that he heard the Prophet {Peace be upon Him} saying:

> "The one subjected to the severest torture on the Day of Judgment shall be the one who either killed a Prophet or the one who was killed by a Prophet, or the one who has killed either of his parents and the one portraying pictures, and a scholar who does not benefit out of his knowledge." (Baihaqi)

It means that the one who portrays pictures, also falls under the category of the major sins and therefore a penalty which is incurred by the murderer of a Messenger shall also be incurred by the one who portrays pictures.

It is narrated by Abu Hurairah {May Allah have mercy on him} that he heard the Prophet {Peace be upon Him} saying:

> "Allah the Almighty says that the most wrong-doer person is the one who makes an effort to create like I do. In case some one boasts of doing that, let him create a particle, a grain or a barley." (Al-Bukhari-Muslim)

It implies that a portrayer (i.e. an artist) surreptitiously claims Divinity. He intends to create things which are the sole prerogative of Allah. He is the most arrogant person and a great liar. Despite the fact that he does not even possess the capability of creating a grain, he is still trying to emulate divinity. An imitator is a condemned person who is accursed by Allah.

The statement of the Prophet {Peace be upon Him} about himself:

It is narrated by Anas {May Allah have mercy on him} that Allah's Messenger {Peace be upon Him} said:

"I do not want you to raise me above the status which Allah has designated for me. I am Muhammad, the son of Abdullah, a slave of Allah and His Messenger." (Razin)[1]

---

[1] The references of this matter are to be found in *Musnad Ahmad* and *At- Tabarani* etc. The following are the words of *Hadith* recorded in *Musnad Ahmad:*

It is narrated by Anas {May Allah have mercy on him} :

"A person said to the Prophet {Peace be upon Him} "You are our chief and the son of our chief!" The Prophet {Peace be upon Him} answered, "You may say so, but you must observe an utmost precaution lest the Satan should play tricks on you and prompts you into the act of exaggerating about me. I am Muhammad, the son of Abdullah and I swear to Allah that I do not like you to uplift me further from the status which Allah has assigned to me (by extolling me to skies

The point which the Prophet {Peace be upon Him} wanted to drive home is that the way the other people, enjoying power and authority (i.e. the celebrities and tycoons), feel gratified and flattered out of being excessively praised, he (the Prophet {Peace be upon Him}) did not like being exaggerated in his praise even in the least. These (so called) great people have nothing to do with the religion of those who lavish praise on them and they little care about whether or not they observe the precepts of their religions. But the Prophet {Peace be upon Him} was so kind and compassionate about his *Ummah* that he was always obsessed with their welfare in terms of religion (i.e. uplifting their moral standards and edifying their religious awakening etc.). When he {Peace be upon Him} knew that the people of his *Ummah* loved him on the immense and cherished that the way the other people, enjoying power and authority (i.e. the celebrities and tycoons), feel gratified and flattered out of being excessively praised, he (the Prophet {Peace be upon Him}) did not like being exaggerated in his praise even in the least. These (so called) great people have nothing to do with the religion of those who lavish praise on them and they little care about whether or not they observe the precepts of their religions. But the Prophet {Peace be upon Him} was so kind and compassionate about his *Ummah* that he was always obsessed with their welfare in terms of religion (i.e. uplifting their moral standards and edifying their religious awakening etc.). When he {Peace be upon Him} knew that the people of his *Ummah* loved him on the immense and cherished their utmost gratitudes for him while also being aware of the fact that in order to oblige their favorites, people often eulogize them by extolling them to the skies, the Prophet {Peace be upon Him} became afraid lest the people should exceed the limits in lavishing praise on him thereby committing a sacrilege towards Allah, because if such a thing happens, their faith shall be utterly destroyed, and it is but imperative that it will also cause a resentment to him (the Prophet {Peace be upon Him}). With a view to this possibility, the Prophet {Peace be upon Him} declared that he disliked exaggeration in his own respect. He {Peace be upon Him} said, "My name is Muhammad {Peace be upon Him}' I am not the creator or sustainer. Like anybody else, I was sired by my father and my honor lies within the status of my being a slave of Allah. The only thing separating me from the common people is that I have the knowledge of the commandments of Allah which the people do not have. Therefore, people should seek the knowledge of Allah's religion from me."

O our *Rabb!* Show Your mercy and blessing upon the one who was sent as a manifestation of mercy for the entire world (i.e. the Prophet {Peace be upon Him}).

O Allah! None but You can understand and reward to the fullest, the tireless efforts which the Prophet {Peace be upon Him} made to teach religion to the ignorant like us.

O Allah, the Exalted, the Supreme! We are none but your helpless slaves! Nothing lies under our

---

through hyperboles)."

A narration of At-Tabarani composes these words:

It is narrated by Husain bin Ali {May Allah have mercy on him} that the Prophet {Peace be upon Him} said:

"Do not raise me any further than what my status is, because Allah has created me as His slave prior to appointing me as His Messenger.'"

control. As You, by Your grace, have made us comprehend and appreciate the meanings of *Shirk* (polytheism) and *Tauhid* (The Oneness of Allah), made us aware about the requirements of *La ilaha ill-Allah,* separated us from among the polytheists and made us purified and among the ones who believe in the Oneness of Allah, we entreat You to similarly teach us, by Your kindness and munificence, the meanings of *Bid'ah* (i.e. innovation in religion) and *Sunnah* (the ways of the Prophet {Peace be upon Him}*),* award us an awareness about the compulsory requirements of pronouncing the *Kalimah "Muhammad Rasulullah. "*

O my *Rabb!* We implore You to be so kind as to separate and distance us from among the apostates and the ones who innovate new things in religion and make us the pure devotees of the creed of the Prophet {Peace be upon Him}and prompt us into being the followers of Qur'an and *Sunnah. Amin.*

Lightning Source UK Ltd.
Milton Keynes UK
UKHW010907080223
416610UK00013B/746